Credit Card Processing for Sales Agents

Edited By Bill Pirtle

Study Guide

**Credit Card Consortia
for Education & Training**

Royal Oak, Michigan

Library of Congress Control Number: 2012916686
ISBN: 9780982611678

Additional copies may be obtained by contacting the publisher. Bulk discounts are also available.

C3ET, Credit Card Consortia for Education and Training, Inc.
P.O. Box 904
Royal Oak, MI 48068
Phone: 734-272-6177
Fax: 888-311-6640
www.creditcardprocessingforsalesagents.com
email: Bill@C3ET.net

Cover design by Identity Graphics Design

Printed in the United States of America

CONTENTS

This study guide complements the book, *Credit Card Processing for Sales Agents* (© 2012 C3ET). A collaborative undertaking, it is the flagship effort on the part of the credit card processing industry to provide standardized curricula for training sales agents.

To test the readers' comprehension of the subject matter, the Study Guide provides the opportunity to practice calculations and sales scenarios. Its insightful questions will aid in skills development and ethical thinking. Suggested "Activities" are provided to enhance study and encourage independent research. The area under "Discussion Topics/Notes" has been left blank in some cases to allow for individual note taking. Some of the topics provided therein will serve as a springboard for the agents' discussions with their particular ISOs.

The Study Guide is customizable, allowing the ISO to use it in its entirety or as sections within specific training programs.

Questions for Chapters 43 and 44 are not included as the authors simply explained their personal experiences in setting up an ISO and your experience may differ.

The contributors to the book have provided a few of the questions provided herein. A substantial portion were written by editors. Every effort has been made to ensure their integrity in augmenting the material. As with *Credit Card Processing for Sales Agents*, the legal topics are for information purposes in general. Specific questions should be referred to an attorney.

QUESTIONS

1-1. Which choice represents one basis point?

  A. .0001

  B. .01%

  C. $0.01 of a $100 transaction

  D. All of the above

1-2. You find that you can save a merchant 35 basis points on his rate. What is the total annual savings for the merchant if his current sales are $25,600 a month?

  A. $1,075.20

  B $107.52

  C. $1,265.85

  D. Not given enough information to answer

1-3. You decide to offer a merchant 0.35% + $0.10 over Interchange. What are the approximate total rates for the following Interchange levels?

  A. 1.65% + $0.10   B. 2.10% + $0.10   C. 1.65% + $0.04   D. 0.05% + $0.22

1-4. For Question 1-3 list a category from the Visa Interchange rate list of April 14, 2012 for each rate and show costs for $10, $50, and $100 transactions.

1-5. For Tiered pricing, who determines whether a category is classified as Qualified, Mid-Qualified, or Non-Qualified?

1-6. True or False: It is possible to save a merchant more by correcting errors in processing than by changing rates.

1-7. According to Deputy Chief Enterprise Risk Officer Adrian Phillips of Visa in a 2009 interview, how many breached companies were found to be PCI compliant at the time of the breach?

1-8. When discussing PCI compliance with a merchant, should you consider PCI as a destination or a journey?

1-9. True or False: You only need to check the effective rate for one statement because it will not change from month to month.

1-10. What factors can skew an effective rate?

1-11. Why does the author suggest that 1% over the Qualified rate is a decent effective rate?

1-12. How do you calculate the effective rate?

1-13. Does the type of merchant make a difference when reviewing the effective rate?

Discussion Topics/Notes

Chapter 3

1-1. D. All of the above

1-2. D. Not given enough information to answer

Explanation: There are over 40 price points that need to be factored in, including the statement fee, transaction fee, PCI fee, annual fee, etc.

1-3.

A. 1.65% + $0.10	B. 2.10% + $0.10	C. 1.65% + $0.04	D. 0.05% + $0.22
0.11% + $0.02	0.11% + $0.02	0.11% + $0.02	0.11% + $0.02
0.35% + $0.10	0.35% + $0.10	0.35% + $0.10	0.35% + $0.10
2.11% + $0.22	2.56% + $0.22	2.11% + $0.16	0.51% + $0.34

1-4.

CPS/Rewards 1	Visa Signature Preferred	CPS/Small Ticket	Regulated Debit
$0.431	$0.476	$0.371	$0.391
$1.275	$1.50	N/A	$0.595
$2.33	$2.78	N/A	$0.85

1-5. Your ISO will determine the bucket into which the Interchange categories should be placed.

1-6. True. Eliminating standards and EIRFs will reduce costs by up to 100 basis points whether priced on Interchange Plus or in a Tiered structure.

1-7. Zero

1-8. PCI is a journey that is continuous. Every day each process must comply with PCI rules to keep information safe. A single failure may result in a breach.

1-9. False. It is almost impossible that the effective rate would be the same from month to month due to the mix of cards accepted and the merchant's volume.

1-10. Annual fees, PCI fees, IRS fees, statement fees (especially with small volume merchants)

1-11. 1% over would take into account other fees assessed for Business and Reward cards and cards that fall to MQ or NQ. The 1% is subjective; you may decide to go higher or lower depending on the merchant's volume or other factors.

1-12. Total fees/Net Sales × 100 = Effective Rate

1-13. Yes, especially since the Durbin Amendment. Higher dollar volume of Regulated Debit can provide opportunity where higher dollar volume of Business Cards might not.

CHAPTER 2
WHAT MAKES UP THE MERCHANTS' COSTS?

QUESTIONS

2-1. If a merchant needs a new terminal, what are the author's two tips?

2-2. Why might a merchant be willing to pay an Application fee or Annual fees?

2-3. Under which pricing structure is it easier to determine your income?

2-4. Which pricing structure will likely earn you more income?

2-5. Are you familiar with the additional fees listed in Chapter 2 that your partner(s) use(s)? Do you know who to ask if you have questions on them?

2-6. What dollar volume would your merchant have to process at 1.79% to avoid a $30 monthly minimum (based on processing fees)?
  A. $1,479.29
  B. $1,675.98
  C. $1,790.00
  D. Cannot determine without transaction cost

2-7. Can you determine the exact dollar volume needed if the Monthly Minimum is based on total profit?
  A. Yes, if the merchant has Tiered pricing
  B. Yes, if the merchant has Interchange Plus pricing
  C. Yes, for both methods
  D. No, for either method

2-8. What do EBB and ERR stand for and why are they controversial in the credit card processing industry?

2-9. Name three possible disadvantages to the merchant for using a "free" terminal from the processor.

2-10. What disadvantages might the sales agent face from providing "free" terminals?

2-11. What is a Chargeback?

2-12. Can a sales agent help a merchant to prevent Chargebacks?

2-13. Your client calls you asking for help with a Retrieval request. Why should you instead refer the client to her processor for assistance?
A. The credit department is experienced in dealing with Chargebacks.
B. You may give out bad information.
C. You risk liability and financial loss if the client loses the Chargeback.
D. All of the above are correct.

2-14. List and discuss the possible reasons for Holds in the following scenarios.

A. An art gallery you sign up has an average ticket of $950 according to the client's last three statements. The highest ticket you see is $4,000. After signing her, she gets a Hold for a sale of $15,000. Why?

B. A sales agent signs a restaurant on October 13. Based on the last six months of statements, its monthly sales averaged $120,000. The average transaction was about $300. October sales were $70,000, November sales were $250,000, and December's were approaching $400,000 with some tickets in the $20,000 range. When the processor held funds, the restaurant went out of business. What happened?

Discussions Topics/Notes

Does your ISO recommend you use monthly minimums in your pricing?

2-1. Sell the merchant the best model that she can afford (it should have EMV capabilities and enough memory for additional services) and show why she should buy from you instead of E-Bay® or Craigslist®.

2-2. When the merchant is pushing for a lower rate, he may be willing to pay a bit up front for the Application or Annual fee. Use tools to help you negotiate and bring some profit even if monthly residual is lower than you would like.

2-3. Interchange Plus

2-4. Tiered

2-5. Check your merchant applications for the fees. Your contact person, sales manager, or leader should have the ISO-specific answers.

2-6. B. $1,675.98

The calculation does not include the transaction fee.

2-7. B. Yes, if the merchant has Interchange Plus pricing.

At IC + 0.25%, the merchant would need $12,000 in sales to avoid a $30 Monthly Minimum.

2-8. EBB is Enhanced Bill Back and ERR is Enhanced Rate Recovery (or Enhanced Recover Reduced). EBB is a process that handles downgrades in the following month, allowing for more profit and confusing 95% of agents who review the statements. ERR allows an agent to be competitive on debit and swipe of basic cards, yet make money in downgraded areas. (Please see Chapter 12 for another view of ERR.)

2-9. 1. higher Batch fee
2. Monthly Minimum fee enforced
3. Annual fees

2-10. Lower upfront profit (profit from sale or lease vs. contract bonus); lower residual split percentage or a much lower residual

2-11. The forced return of a credit card purchase without the recovery of product or service sold

2-12. Yes, an agent can help the merchant prevent Chargebacks by properly training him on the card brand rules, on proper point of sale procedures, and establishing a clearly defined return policy.

2-13. All of the above are correct.

Referring the client to her processor's credit department is not a cop out and it is not admitting that you do not know the answer. The processor has experts on Chargebacks and can give the client fast, accurate responses. You could give the client the exact right information and still risk being sued if she loses the sale. Put the client in touch with her processor immediately.

2-14.

A. Do not make the mistake of just using the statements to complete the application. Talk to your prospect; ask questions. In this case, the agent never asked for the client's highest sale amount; he assumed it was $4,000 based on the last few statements. Further, he did not ask for the total volume but estimated it based on the three statements. For this client, the last three statements represented slow months. The sales agent made monthly and high sales predictions based on the slow months and the higher sales surprised the processor. The solution is to give the underwriters complete information so that they expect the higher sales months and high ticket items.

B. The sales agent did not ask the right questions. Picture a nice restaurant that serves its own wines. The agent saw the average transactions, but did not anticipate Thanksgiving and Christmas parties. By asking about holiday sales, the sales agents can provide the underwriters with a clearer picture. Also, by advising merchants to fax or call their processor when they have excessive sales alerts the processor of a large transaction so its underwriter can request a signed invoice. Holds are caused by surprising the processor, which in turn causes the processor to anticipate a loss. The holding of funds can cripple a business. Ask better questions.

CHAPTER 3
WHAT MERCHANTS ARE PAYING FOR

3-1. True or False: Customers are willing to pay more for great customer service.

3-2. If you sell the merchant on price, how will you lose the merchant?

3-3. How can a merchant increase sales by accepting credit cards?

3-4. According to MasterCard, how much will sales increase when a merchant decides to accept credit cards?

3-5. Give two examples of why credit card funding is considered to be a loan.

3-6. What single factor determines the rate more than any other according to Pirtle?

3-7. List the fraud prevention tools present on a MasterCard Debit Card.

3-8. What are the brands' programs called for online fraud prevention?

3-9. What fraud prevention tool does the author believe is critical for every website?

What services or tools of your ISO help to set you apart from your competition?

ANSWERS

3-1. True. If customers did not want service, stores like Nordstrom's would not exist.

3-2. On price. If you make it about how much you can save the merchant, you will lose him to the first competitor who is willing to make less than you make on him.

3-3. Impulse sales. Much like the example given in the book regarding upgrades on a computer, impulse sales are when a customer decides to make an unplanned purchase.

3-4. The MasterCard finding was that sales will increase by 56%.

3-5. 1. personal guarantee is mandated on the application

2. Chargebacks

3-6. Risk. Risks include the customer not paying, the business folding with Chargebacks coming back, and risks associated with fraud.

3-7.
- the hologram
- the first four numbers under the imprint
- logo on the card; layout of the numbers on the face
- the signature field reading "VOID" if tampered with
- the last four numbers of the card in the signature field
- the three-digit security code (CVC, Visa calls it the CVV2)

3-8. Verified by Visa and MasterCard Secure Code

3-9. The AVS or Address Verification System. Without the AVS, fraudsters can use your credit card to deliver anywhere in the world.

CHAPTER 4

CARD ACCEPTANCE GUIDELINES—WHAT MERCHANTS NEED TO KNOW

4-1. List the reasons why merchants should not request an ID except when the customer's signature does not match the card.

4-2. True or False: By not signing a credit card, a cardholder is less likely to encounter fraud if his card is stolen.

4-3. Why is it not a good idea to circle the amount, tip, or signature on a credit card receipt?

4-4. Why do the card brands penalize merchants who are caught recording the three-digit security number?

4-5. Why is it a good idea to have terminals programmed to request the last four numbers of the credit card?

4-6. Why is AVS a must have when shipping is involved?

4-7. Must a merchant have SSL on a website that accepts credit cards?

4-8. Give five reasons as to why a merchant should accept credit cards.

4-9. How does Pirtle suggest that merchants account for card processing fees?

4-10. What does EIRF mean and what causes it?

4-11. What is the term used when a merchant runs the transactions of another merchant? Why is doing this a problem?

4-12. Is it considered factoring when someone with five websites uses a single merchant account?

4-13. A merchant mistakenly runs a $10,000 transaction instead of a $100 transaction. Do you tell him to void it or do a return? Why?

4-14. What is the maximum recommended amount that a merchant, using his own credit card, should run through his store's credit card terminal?

Discussions Topics/Notes

4-1.
- Cashiers are not trained to properly review an ID.
- Requiring an ID to complete a transaction violates card brand rules.
- Identification only shows that the ID bears the same name as that on the credit card; it does not prove ownership of the card (for example, a child or cousin of the cardholder might share the same name).
- Asking for ID seems like a shortcut to the merchant but it causes more fraudulent transactions.
- The cashier is only verifying that the ID carries the same name as the card without regard for identifying features.
- If the card was stolen, the ID was too.
- Properly reviewing an ID for each credit card customer will greatly slow down the line compared to using Visa's Point-of-Sale Rules, which typically take 5 seconds.
- Following Visa's rules will cut 74% of fraud.
- Checking for an ID will not protect the merchant from a Chargeback.

4-2. False. By not signing, he is more likely to suffer fraud. Visa's Point-of-Sale Rules reduce fraud by 74% when followed. Advise your merchants that by the rules, an unsigned card is invalid and the customer will lose the Chargeback.

4-3. It can corrupt the receipt. Since a merchant needs to photocopy the receipt to fax it for a Retrieval request, any stray marks or circles can distort the receipt making it unreadable and unusable in defense of the Chargeback.

4-4. It is prohibited to record the number, no matter how well it is secured.

4-5. Requesting the cashier to enter the last four numbers on the card is a great way to detect cards that have had their magnetic stripes reprogrammed. If there is no match, the terminal will refuse the sale and save the merchant a Chargeback and lost product.

4-6. The Address Verification System compares the street address and zip code to what the customer has on record as his billing address or authorized shipping address with his bank. By using AVS and programming the gateway not to approve without an AVS match, the merchant will reduce fraud.

4-7. This is a trick question, where the answer is not necessarily cut and dry. At the point where the card numbers are entered, it must be a secure page. However, if the merchant is using a Visa Certified Gateway where the shopping cart moves the sale to the gateway for card number entry, then the merchant's site does not need the SSL.

4-8.
1. showing customers that the merchant is reputable
2. giving protections to customers that a "guarantee" cannot
3. giving customers a choice of payment types
4. allowing customers to make payments over time while giving the business owner all of the money now (minus processing fees)
5. for rental properties, it increases the percentage of on-time payments; it helps tenants pay on time, saving them late fees

4-9. Increase prices by 5% and do not give discounts for cash or check.

4-10. Electronic Interchange Reimbursement Fee. It is caused by errors in the processing, such as including tips and late or irregular batch times among others. The MasterCard equivalent term is Standard.

4-11. The term is factoring. It is a problem for several reasons:
- It can be used for fraud.
- The processor cannot evaluate risk for the aggregated merchant.
- Chargebacks will occur for the processing merchant as the customer will not recognize the transaction (the processing merchant loses money while the aggregate merchant keeps the sale and funds).

4-12. It is if each site has different names and/or product types. However, if a single MCC code is used (and only one is needed), and all sites list that XYZ Company will appear on the statement, then the answer is no.

4-13. Void before the batch time. If a transaction has batched, have the merchant contact the processor for options. The last option is to return. Train your merchants to void mistakes. A void removes the approved transaction before the batch, so merchant will only pay the transaction fee. If returned, it is possible that the merchant will pay processing fees on both the sale and return; even if within the same batch.

4-14. $1.00, but only for the purpose of testing the equipment. The card brands consider it fraud to use your own card in your business' terminal. The reason is that you are creating a cash advance without paying the issuer for the advance.

5-1. True or False: On IC+ accounts that qualify for Small Ticket Interchange, a swiped credit card cost will be lower for a $10 transaction than a Regulated Debit.

5-2. Are credit card processors or card brands responsible for the high cost of gasoline, in the opinion of the author?

5-3. Name three of the biggest winners since enactment of the Durbin Amendment.

5-4. What three business classes are mostly unaffected by the Durbin Amendment?

5-5. Who are the two losers since enactment of the Durbin Amendment?

5-6. Do you agree with the author on the overall effect of the Durbin Amendment? Why?

What is your ISO's opinion on Durbin?

ANSWERS

5-1. True.

Regulated Debit Cost on $10.00 Transaction			Small Ticket Cost on $10 Transaction	
Interchange	0.05% + $0.22 = $0.225		1.55% + $0.04 = $0.195	
D&A	0.11% + $0.02 = $0.031		0.11% + $0.02 = $0.031	
IC+	0.25% + $0.10 = $0.125		0.25% + $0.10 = $0.125	
Total	0.41% + $0.34 = $0.381		1.91% + $0.16 = $0.351	

5-2. No. Branded gas stations are required to buy processing from the brand or the jobber at higher fees than are available to gas stations not so required.

5-3. Any of the following are correct.
- Big Box retailers like WalMart, Home Depot, Lowes
- agents using tiered pricing
- processors where agents use Tiered pricing
- Dick Durbin
- associations like the NACS and the NRF are also winners as they have a lobbying victory to use to gain more members

5-4. Any of the following are correct.
- the card brands (make money on D&A, which were not disturbed by amendment)
- processors using IC+ pricing
- sales agents using IC+ pricing
- banks under $10 billion in assets

5-5.
- consumers
- banks over $10 billion in assets

5-6. Answer is subjective

6-1. Must all merchants who accept MasterCard and Visa be compliant with PCI DSS?

6-2. Must all merchants undergo an onsite PCI audit?

6-3. Do MasterCard and Visa require all merchants to validate PCI by completing a security assessment questionnaire?

6-4. Are acquirers liable for fines resulting from merchant data breaches?

6-5. How do acquirers pass on these fines to merchants?

6-6. Are all merchants required by MasterCard and Visa to undergo quarterly network scans?

6-7. Do acquirers require scans for all merchants?

6-8. Are acquirers required to undergo onsite PCI audits?

6-9. Are MasterCard/Visa issuers required to be PCI compliant?

6-10. What requirements exist for payment applications?

6-11. How many PCI Data Security requirements are there?

Does your ISO require scanning? How often?

ANSWERS

6-1. Yes, all must comply with PCI DSS.

6-2. No. Only merchant levels 1-2 for Visa and merchant levels 1-3 for MasterCard need to undergo an onsite PCI audit.

6-3. No. Only merchant levels 1-3 must validate PCI. Acquirers may require validation at their option.

6-4. Yes

6-5. Per language in the merchant contract, a merchant is required to compensate the acquirer for fines received due to the merchant's actions.

6-6. No. Only merchant levels 1-2 for Visa and merchant levels 1-3 for MasterCard need an onsite PCI audit.

6-7. Many acquirers do require all merchants to undergo scanning.

6-8. Acquirers who process > 300, 000 transactions annually must undergo onsite audits.

6-9. Yes, they must comply with PCI DSS.

6-10. Payment applications must comply with Visa PA-DSS to help prevent storage of sensitive card data.

6-11. There are 12 requirements covering six areas.

7-1. What are the dates for Visa's fraud liability shifts?

7-2. What does EMV stand for?

7-3. Who are the partners of EMVCo LLC?

7-4. In VeriFone's whitepaper dated October of 2011, what is the purpose of the digital keys?

7-5. Why do VeriFone executives believe that large merchants will jump on board to acquire EMV-capable terminals?

7-6. What North American country currently uses EMV cards?

7-7. What is another term for EMV cards?

7-8. What is one problem resulting from Europe and the U.S. using different systems?

7-9. Will online shoppers be able to verify their cards?

7-10. What does the author suggest agents do?

ANSWERS

7-1. October 1, 2015 for all POS systems except fuel dispensers, which is October 1, 2017

7-2. EuroPay International, MasterCard, Visa

7-3. MasterCard, Visa, AMEX, and JCB

7-4. Digital keys on smart cards prevent cloning of chip cards.

7-5. Visa's Technology Innovation Program (TIP), which eliminates the requirement for eligible merchants (level one) to annually validate their compliance with the PCI Data Security Standard for any year in which at least 75% of the merchant's Visa transactions originate from chip-enabled terminals.

7-6. Canada

7-7. Smart Cards

7-8. While banks are now issuing EMV cards to the more affluent international travelers, many American and European travelers may not be able to use their cards while travelling overseas.

7-9. Yes, Barclays' PINsentry is one of many devices. A consumer can plug it into her computer and place the card into the chip reader to verify presence of the card while online.

7-10. Sell, place, lease, or rent EMV-capable terminals now so you will not have to go back in two years and sell an upgrade.

8-1. What specific action can remove personal liability from an MLS?
    A. Being ethical in dealing with merchants
    B. Giving clients fair pricing
    C. By incorporating
    D. All of the above
    E. None of the above

8-2. True or False: Atlas believes that no agent should be exclusive.

8-3. True or False: Any default by an ISO will allow the MLS to justifiably breach the Non-Solicitation Clause to move clients.

8-4. True or False: Only ISOs need to be concerned about partners taking clients under the Non-Solicitation Clause.

8-5. Define a "buy rate" deal.

8-6. Define a "revenue-share" deal.

8-7. Which is the better revenue-share deal for an MLS?
    A. 50-50
    B. 60-40
    C. 80-20
    D. 100% over Interchange
    E. Not enough information to answer the question

8-8. Which is a possible reason for an MLS to lose a "lifetime residual"?
    A. Merchant is not generating residuals for the ISO.
    B. ISO has sold the portfolio.
    C. The MLS has been terminated for cause.
    D. All of the above
    E. None of the above

8-9. In case of a dispute between the MLS and the ISO regarding non-payment of residuals, which party, in Atlas' experience, typically has the stronger case?

8-10. In which situation is the MLS *not* liable for a merchant Chargeback or fraud?
    A. Where the MLS is involved in the fraud
    B. Where the MLS boards a merchant he knew he shouldn't
    C. Where the MLS had no role in the loss
    D. Where the MLS had no role in the loss and carries no liability for the loss

8-11. True or False: An MLS who has incorporated will have no personal liability to the ISO.

8-12. True or False: Even if you are incorporated, you need to be registered with the card brands to market under your business name.

8-13. True or False: Agent agreements cannot be negotiated. It is take it or leave it.

Discussions Topics/Notes

8-1. C. By incorporating.

A & B are good qualities, but cannot remove liability. Be mindful that there is the possibility of losing the protection in cases of fraud or by not properly running the incorporated entity.

8-2. False. Atlas believes that the exclusivity clause can be used to negotiate a better split and other benefits.

8-3. False. Consult an attorney before breaching this clause. It may result in a breach of contract lawsuit against you and can be very expensive.

8-4. False. MLS should be wary of ISOs who solicit clients that they brought to the ISO for the purpose of cutting the MLS out of earned residuals.

8-5. A buy-rate deal allows an MLS to keep 100% of proceeds beyond a minimum pricing level established by the ISO.

8-6. Revenue-share deals are where the ISO and MLS share revenue from an account based on pre-defined percentages. Revenue is split once certain minimums are taken, for instance BIN fees.

8-7. E. Not enough information to answer the question

Look beyond the split percentages to see what is netted out as expenses before the split.

8-8. D. All of the above

The reality is that there are no true lifetime residuals. "The lifetime of a given residual payment will depend on the wording of the MLS agreement and the extent to which the MLS and the ISO honor their respective obligations under the agreement."

8-9. The case is made stronger by the extent to which they are honest in their dealings with one other.

8-10. D. Where the MLS had no role in the loss and carries no liability for loss.

Not only must the MLS have no role in the loss, but his or her contract must state that there is no MLS liability for losses.

8-11. False. If the Agent Agreement carries a personal guarantee, then even incorporation will not protect the MLS from losses to the ISO.

8-12. True. Unless registered with the card brands, marketing must be in the name of the registered ISO for whom the MLS is selling.

8-13. False. It can be negotiated and it is recommended that an industry attorney is used.

9-1. What are the three areas of potential impact to the industry?

9-2. Where does the author say an MLS should go for specific equipment questions?

9-3. What are some of the trade publications outlined in the chapter?

9-4. Which publication is best for you to obtain?

9-5. List some industry blogs and online newsletters.

9-6. What do the authors think of online forums?

Activities

- Review and sign up to receive a few trade publications.
- Review some of the available blogs and online newsletters.
- Go to www.greensheet.com and register on the site. Then use for the forum.

ANSWERS

9-1.
1. Legislation
2. Security
3. Technology

9-2. The website of the vendor in question

9-3.
The Green Sheet
Digital Transactions
Transaction Trends
ISO & Agent
The Nilson Report
Transaction World

9-4. The best sources depend upon your goals and whether you are an MLS or an ISO.

9-5.
"Selling Prepaid"
"Inside Microfinance"
The Strawhecker Group
"The Navigator"
Glenbrook Partners

9-6. The forums can be useful when used correctly.

10-1. What makes up Paul J. Meyer's S.M.A.R.T. goals?

10-2. Is "more sales" a legitimate goal? Why?

10-3. Which of the following items represent specific goals?
   A. Increasing sales by 30% within one year
   B. Increasing sales by 2 per month
   C. Buying a new car
   D. Buying a 2013 Cadillac XLR

10-4. What method does Pirtle suggest to measure your goals?

10-5. Why are attainable goals critical?

10-6. What is the difference between attainable and realistic goals?

10-7. What is a benefit of having multiple goals set over various points of time (for example, one month, six months, one year, five years)?

10-8. Betty continually set new goals and recorded all of her activity. How did this help her?

Create specific business and personal goals for the following times:

One Week

One Month

One Quarter

Six Months

One Year

Two Years

Five Years

ANSWERS

10-1.
- Specific
- Measurable
- Attainable
- Realistic
- Time bound

10-2. "More sales" is not a legitimate goal. It is not specific. Besides, if you have one more sale, you have "more sales."

10-3. A, B, and D are all specific goals.

10-4. Record everything that you do.

10-5. Attainable goals are critical because if you continually fail to hit your goals, you will lose faith. Make them hard, but make them within your reach.

10-6. Attainable goals may be hit but realistic goals are expected to be hit.

10-7. One benefit is that the outcomes of shorter-term goals can help to modify longer term goals. For instance, if you continually exceed your short-term goals, you can challenge yourself by increasing your longer-term goals.

10-8. By recording all of her activities, Betty learned what things worked best for her and modified her sales routine to best suit her skills.

11-1. _____, _____, and _____ are just a few of the names associated with unethical and even criminal acts.

11-2. On the other side, history gives us _____, _____, and _____.

11-3. What is a problem with ethics?

11-4. Why does the author tie ethics to value?

11-5. Which widget scenario does Caine believe is more ethical and why?

11-6. Which scenario do you believe is more ethical and why?

11-7. True or False: Mr. Caine seems to be saying that the MLS is not being ethical if pricing an account so low that he or she cannot profit enough to remain in the industry.

11-8. Under Caine's definition of ethics, if you sold a merchant decent rate with a lease on a terminal for $100/month that included a gift card program that created $2,000 of additional sales per month, would this be an ethical sale? Why or why not?

11-9. In the early days, what were some common issues with card processing?

11-10. True or False: Caine believes that it is ethical for an MLS to charge $100/month on a lease where a merchant is saving $200/month in processing and realizing even more in overhead efficiencies.

11-11. What does the author surmise would have occurred with a low markup at the time where ISOs first entered the arena?

11-12. You cannot be _____ if you do not _____.

11-13. True or False: If fraudulent action results in the same pricing as another's ethical pricing, then that action is ethical.

11-14. True or False: Larger ISOs can get lower Interchange rates than smaller ones.

11-15. The majority of unethical behavior, specifically concerning sales and marketing tactics, is the result of two things: _____ and _____.

11-16. What are the six steps to practice "value-added" selling?

11-17. True or False: There is currently no government oversight or regulation controlling credit card processing activity.

Discussions Topics/Notes

11-1. Ponzi, Madoff, and Enron

11-2. Socrates, Aristotle, and Solomon

11-3. One person's "ethical good" may be another's evil.

11-4. He believes that the value provided determines whether the cost is ethical.

11-5. Scenario #3 is more ethical, because both the seller and the buyer have the maximum value. The seller receives the maximum return and the buyer receives an exclusive arrangement.

11-6. The answer is for the reader alone to determine as it is subjective.

11-7. True. Assume that a merchant signs with you over a promise of quality service and you price the account so low that you cannot make enough in the industry to remain in it. The merchant is virtually hung out to dry without the service he was promised. In this case, the pricing is unethical because not only are you forced out of the business, but you do not provide the value that you promised.

11-8. Under Caine's definition of ethics, the agent needs to derive a good income for providing value to the merchant. For the question, the lease would cost $4,800 for four years while bringing in an additional $96,000 in sales. Yes, this would be an ethical setup.

11-9.

- Higher rates (3-4% common)
- Needed to imprint slips
- Needed to look up in stolen card list
- List was always outdated
- Slips needed to be taken to the bank.
- Floor limits
- Losses

11-10. True. Since the MLS helped the merchant to cut both costs and expenses, it was proper to receive a benefit of that. Especially when you consider that early on in the industry the MLS did not receive residuals, he received only the commission on the equipment.

11-11. The ISOs probably would not have had much incentive to aggressively grow.

11-12. Ethical, provide value

11-13. False. Fraudulent behavior and misrepresentation is always unethical. It is not the pricing that determines whether or not a deal is ethical; it is the value brought into the equation and how the signature was obtained.

11-14. False. Interchange is the rate paid to the issuing bank. The issuing bank is not about to offer discounts to anyone. Every single ISO and processor pays the exact same Interchange rate and Dues & Assessments.

11-15. Insufficient sales training and dishonest sales representatives looking for a quick buck

11-16.
1. Properly identify your prospect.
2. Provide a high-level overview of what you are offering, including features and benefits.
3. Conduct a "needs analysis."
4. Present your solutions and benefits in an organized and professional manner.
5. Close the sale by honestly overcoming any raised objections.
6. Ensure satisfaction after the sale and follow up with the merchant on a regular basis.

11-17. True. Outside of existing laws covering fraud, there is no regulation of the card processing industry.

12-1. Sales professionals equipped with the knowledge and tools to assist their merchants in _____ wherever possible are able to provide better service and therefore improve merchant retention.

12-2. Define Interchange.

12-3. Who pays the Interchange to the issuer?
A. The customer
B. The merchant
C. The acquirer
D. The card brand

12-4. True or False: New Interchange categories were created to incent issuers for categories like Rewards cards.

12-5. Why do the card brands provide lower "emerging market" rates to some merchants?

12-6. Table 12-1 illustrates _____ specific and _____ specific Interchange categories.

12-7. Name four variables for determining an Interchange rate.

12-8. Which is a type of a Tiered pricing structures?
A. 2-Tiered
B. 3-Tiered
C. 4-Tiered
D. 8-Tiered
E. All are possible types among others.

12-9. Which type of Tiered pricing do you think would typically create the most profit for the MLS?

12-10. Who controls which "bucket" an Interchange category falls into?

12-11. Name some Pass-through Plus pricing methods.

12-12. What does ERR stand for?

12-13. What is the ERR cost for a $100 transaction with a 1.74% + $0.25 Qualified rate, a 0.35% ERR fee, and swiping a card listed as Commercial Retail (2.30% + $0.10)? (Show the steps taken to calculate your answer.)

12-14. Referring to question 12-13, what is the total rate charged to the merchant?
A. 3.10%
B. 2.80%
C. 2.85%
D. 2.95%

12-15. What "new" fee should agents look for on statements of Tiered merchants?

12-16. Under the Fed rule brought by the Durbin Amendment, 0.05% + $0.21 (plus 1 cent for fraud prevention programs) is the Regulated Debit rate for all of the following, except:
A. Small ticket
B. Keyed entry
C. Internet with no AVS attempted
D. EIRF transactions
E. None of the above
F. All of the above

Discussions Topics/Notes

ANSWERS

12-1. Reducing downgrades

12-2. Interchange is the fee set by the card brands payable to the issuing bank for use of the credit or debit card.

12-3. C. The acquirer

The processor (acquirer) pays the Interchange. The amount charged to the merchant should account for Interchange and Dues & Assessments.

12-4. True.

12-5. To penetrate markets that had not accepted credit cards previously, including utilities, fast food, and parking.

12-6. Card, merchant

12-7.
- Who issued the card?
- Are there rewards?
- Is the card foreign or domestic?
- Does the transaction qualify for any special programs?
- Is the card being swiped?
- Is the merchant set up properly to identify the transaction correctly?

12-8. E. All are possible types among others.

12-9. Typically, the fewer the tiers, the higher the profit opportunity is. The 2-Tiers are simply Qualified and Non-Qualified, thus it is easy for all but a few categories to fall to Non-Qualified. With an 8-Tiered system, you have Qualified, Mid-Qualified, Non-Qualified, and Rewards in both credit and debit levels. In an 8-Tiered system, there are categories between along with lower debit categories.

12-10. The processor

12-11.
- Pass-through plus percentage
- Pass-through plus per-item transaction fee
- Pass-through plus per-item authorization fee
- Pass-through plus percentage and per-item fee

12-12. Enhanced Recovery Reduced

12-13.
1. $100 \times 1.74\%$ Qualified rate + $0.25 = $1.99
2. Subtract CPS Retail from Commercial Retail, so $1.54\% - 2.30\% \times $100 = 0.76\%$ or $0.76.

3. ERR surcharge: $100 × 0.35%= $0.35

4. Add the total fees: $1.99 + $0.76 + $0.35= $3.10

12-14. C. 2.85%

The total rate would be 2.85% plus a $0.25 transaction fee.

12-15. Dues & Assessments. While they have always appeared on Pass-through Plus (also called Interchange Plus) statements, many ISOs have recently added them to Tiered statements.

12-16. E. None of the above

No matter how processed, Regulated Debit card Interchange is constant.

13-1. Qualified transactions are commonly referred to as:
A. Swiped transactions
B. Keyed transactions
C. Corporate card transactions
D. Elite Card transactions

13-2. True or False: All processors place card types in the same Qualified or Non-Qualified bundles.

13-3. Net sales
A. Includes credit card Chargebacks
B. Includes discount due
C. Includes credit card returns
D. Does not include credit card returns

13-4. If the discount paid is zero, you can assume:
A. The merchant is on a daily discount.
B. The merchant is on a monthly discount.
C. The merchant is paying a higher rate.
D. The merchant is paying a lower rate.

13-5. True or False: Analyzing a Pass-thru statement requires two months of consecutive statements.

13-6. 1.79% is equal to _____.
A. 0.0179
B. 0.00179
C. 0.000179
D. None of the above

13-7. Average ticket is _____ , based on 3,691 transactions and volume of $125,000.
   A. $2.95
   B. $295.00
   C. $33.87
   D. $338.66

13-8. Additional fees on a statement can include:
   A. Monthly fees
   B. Per item fees
   C. TIN fees
   D. All of the above

13-9. Online Debit is to _____ as Offline Debit is to _____ .
   A. Credit, pin number
   B. Visa, Interlink
   C. Pin number, credit
   D. None of the above

13-10. A large number of Non-Qualified transactions may indicate:
   A. The merchant processes debit cards.
   B. The merchant processes corporate cards.
   C. The merchant is on a daily discount.
   D. The merchant has pass-thru pricing
   E. The merchant has a high number of processing errors (EIRFs and standards).

Discussion Topics/Notes

13-1.   A. Swiped transactions

13-2.   False

13-3.   C: Includes credit card returns

13-4.   A. The merchant is on a daily discount.

13-5.   B. False

13-6.   A. 0.0179

13-7.   C. $33.87

13-8.   D. All of the above

13-9.   C. Pin number, credit

13-10. Both B and E are correct. Many will stop looking if they see corporate cards but a large number of EIRFs will allow you to save the merchant money while maintaining or even increasing the merchant's rate.

14-1. Does the MLS need to understand the switch to be successful?

14-2. Fortney defines the switch as the "point whereby the communication between the _____ and the _____work is facilitated."

14-3. Explain the payment cycle.

14-4. In almost every case, the authorization vendor has _____ connectivity options.

14-5. Fortney states that there are about five major authorization vendors who have switches. Name them.

14-6. In Question 14-5, what is the significant difference between two of the companies versus the other three?

14-7. True or False: Operating your own switch gives you better Interchange rates from the card brands.

14-8. True or False: Different switches each have different capabilities.

14-9. True or false? Direct access via dial to the authorization vendor is no faster or slower than use of the switch.

Activities

1. Research switches and platforms and create a list of five where you know the features.

2. Ask your ISO(s) which switches and platforms it can use and what is recommended.

Discussions Topics/Notes

14-1.   No, but understanding switches can help specific merchants in specific situations.

14-2.   Merchant, card association (card brand)

14-3.   The payment cycle consists of both the authorization vendor (front end) and the acquirer (also known as the processor or backend).

14-4.   Two

14-5.
  • First Data
  • Global
  • TSYS
  • Clearent
  • Heartland

14-6.   First Data, Global, and TSYS are used by multiple registered ISOs. Clearent and Heartland operate their own switches.

14-7.   False. As stated earlier, Interchange is constant, regardless of size or the processor or acquirer. There may be fees assessed by the processor or acquirer to the ISOs that process through, but those would be on top of the standard Interchange.

14-8.   True. First Data, for instance, has multiple switches including Nashville, North, South, Buypass, Compass, and Omaha. Buypass works with online processing with Level 2 & 3 while Omaha can be used for next-day funding.

14-9.   False. Utilizing a switch can include processing via IP address, which will expedite transactions and settlements for the merchant.

15-1. What is PCI?

15-2. Where can you find information about PCI?

15-3. Who manages the PCI-DSS?

15-4. Why should you care?

15-5. What is the PCI-SAQ?

15-6. How often must an SAQ be completed?

15-7. What is the PCI-DSS *not*?

15-8. What are the six actions every merchant needs to take for PCI compliance?

15-9. The focus of PCI is on _____, _____, and _____. So, if the merchant includes that in his policy, then he will be in good shape.

15-10. It is recommended that the merchant include specific terms in his written information security policy. What are they?

15-11. List the six items that Janet recommends for the Training Manual.

15-12. What is the definition of "Incident" for your merchants and why must an Incident Response Plan include this definition?

15-13. What is the suggested order for reporting incidents?

15-14. Which of the following statements is true?
    A. PCI compliance means that you will never suffer a breach.
    B. PCI compliance is only a snapshot at one point in time.
    C. PCI compliance is not a destination, but a journey.
    D. You only need to be concerned with PCI once a year.

Discussion Topics/Notes

15-1. "The PCI Data Security Standard represents a common set of industry tools and measurements to help ensure the safe handling of sensitive information."

15-2. The official PCI website is https://www.pcisecurityStandard.org/. Every processor also provides information about PCI for its merchants.

15-3. The PCI-Security Standard Council establishes the standard. The card networks enforce the standard through their acquiring bank partners.

15-4. Merchants, processors, and ISOs who do not comply with the PCI-DSS suffer financial and reputational costs that can be so severe that it puts some out of business.

15-5. The PCI-SSC has created a process for merchants to demonstrate their compliance with the Standard. The document is called a Self-Assessment Questionnaire (PCI-SAQ).

There are several versions of the SAQ based upon how customer payments are accepted (e.g., face to face or via internet). Each merchant is told by his or her processor which version to complete.

15-6. An SAQ must be completed annually.

15-7. PCI is not a process for eliminating the risk associated with a loss of payment card information. It is a standard used as a baseline for evaluating how well companies are protecting payment card information.

PCI is not designed to protect the merchant. It is designed to protect cardholders and the banks that issue payment cards.

PCI is not easy. It is not easy to understand; it is not easy to follow; it is not easy to maintain. And, most of all, it is not easy to protect merchant organizations from the costs associated with a PCI violation. However, it is manageable by following the guidance in Chapter 15.

15-8.
- Conduct a technology audit annually.
- Create an information security policy.
- Develop a procedures manual for secure handling of information.
- Prepare a training manual and train all employees.
- Identify all service providers and modify the needed contract language.
- Develop an incident response plan.

15-9. Prevention, detection, and reaction

15-10.
- Payment card information
- Service provider
- Personnel or covered individuals
- Access to payment card information
- Payment card environment
- Incident or event for the purpose of escalating issues to management

15-11.
1. A description of the topic to be offered
2. The target audience for the training
3. A description of how the training will be presented (self-taught or by instructor)
4. A schedule for when the training will be offered
5. The materials used for the training
6. Documentation used for confirming that training is complete

15-12. The plan must include the definition of an incident specific to the merchant because the definition varies from merchant to merchant.

15-13.
1. Management or business owner
2. Attorney
3. Accountant
4. IT support expert
5. Processor/sales representative
6. Law enforcement
7. Card brands/networks

15-14. B & C are true. Even if a merchant is fully compliant today, there may be a breach tomorrow if a policy is not followed.

16-1. In the example given by Felts, with the penny doubling every day for 31 days, what would you have at 21 days?

16-2. What does the penny example have to do with anything?

16-3. Without removing what is _____ the canoe from being harvested, you will forever have nothing more than a _____.

16-4. A million-dollar portfolio is achieved when the portfolio yields a residual of _____ to _____ per month when a certain condition is reached.

16-5. The multiple will vary depending on the mix of contracts from 18-40 times. What multiple is needed for a million-dollar portfolio if the current residual is $40,000 per month?

16-6. To guarantee a $1,000,000 sale on a portfolio of unknown mix, what is the minimum monthly residual needed based on the range given in Question 16-4.

16-7. According to Felts, if you have _____ contract approvals per month at _____ residuals per merchant, you would be earning $3,600 per month after 12 months.

16-8. How many approved applications per month are needed at $30 income each to be at $9,000 per month in residuals after 12 months?

16-9. What is your residual for the 12th month if you sign 10 accounts per month and your average residual is $50? What is it if you sign 25 accounts per month?

16-10. What variable is not taken in account for in the calculations in Question 16-9 and how should an agent account for this?

16-11. Who can help you create the formula that is best for your specific situation?

16-12. Why is setting sales goals important?

16-13. According to Felts, what are the 10 keys to unlock your million-dollar portfolio?

16-14. Zig Ziglar said, "You were born to win, but to be a winner you must _____ to win, _____ to win, and _____ to win."

16-15. Which ISO is most likely to help an agent acquire a million-dollar portfolio?

Activity

Name a few things preventing you from being the most successful agent that you can be. What will you do to overcome or fix that?

Discussion Topics/Notes

ANSWERS

16-1. $10,385.76

16-2. As an agent sells more accounts her residuals will grow in a similar fashion. For example, if she signs three her first month and makes $80 in residuals on each, her first monthly residual check could be $240. If she signed three additional accounts in the next month, her next residual check would be for $480. By signing more accounts with higher volumes, she could make a lot of money in this business because residuals will continue to grow each month as she adds accounts.

16-3. Preventing, tree

16-4. $25,000 to $55,555

16-5. A 25× payout on a $40,000-a-month residual results in a $1,000,000 payout.

16-6. The range given was 18-40× based on the contract mix. If the mix is unknown, assume the worst at 18× and strive to hit $55,555.

16-7. Ten, $30

16-8. 25

16-9. $6,000, $15,000

16-10. Attrition (merchants leaving). The remedy is to sign enough additional accounts to replace those merchants that leave.

16-11. Your relationship manager or your processor/ISO can help you.

16-12. It is much easier to hit a goal like developing a million-dollar portfolio by breaking the long-term goal into manageable segments and then staying on target.

16-13.
1. Make a specific decision coupled with unwavering determination.
2. Create a plan of action.
3. Develop great processing and VAR relationships.
4. Secure great contracts that protect all parties involved, including you.
5. Create a marketing plan; determine how will you develop leads.
6. Develop professional marketing materials.
7. Perfect your presentation.
8. Provide excellent service.
9. Strive for ongoing education, training, and personal development.
10. Run the numbers, review them frequently, and make them concrete.

16-14. Plan, prepare, expect

16-15. It depends entirely upon the specific agent and advisor/relationship manager of the ISO.

CHAPTER 17
UNDERWRITING AND FRAUD

17-1. What is KYC and what is its significance?

17-2. Each person hired or affiliated should have a _____ to verify that he is who he says he is and that his history is consistent with your expectations.

17-3. What two departments can cost an ISO through fraud perpetrated by inside help?

17-4. True or False: ISOs and processors have the same duty to protect personal merchant information as merchants have to protect cardholders' information.

17-5. The three basic levels of businesses are _____, _____, and _____.

17-6. Why do ISOs review business and owner information so carefully?

17-7. Why is a merchant's credit score less critical for card-present transaction accounts than for Internet or MOTO accounts?

17-8. What role does the MCC/SIC play in fraud analysis?

17-9. What other role does MCC/SIC play in underwriting?

17-10. In April of 2011, PokerStars and Full Tilt Poker were shut down by the FBI and had their accounts frozen. What are the two possible causes from an ISO's viewpoint?

17-11. What are some further ramifications for the ISO in the case of Question 17-10?

17-12. True or False: Reserves are just a way to make life difficult for problem merchants.

Activity

Ask your ISO contacts how you can deliver clean applications and help reduce fraud from their perspective. Remember, if your ISO goes under because of fraud, your residuals will stop.

Discussion Topics/Notes

17-1. Know Your Customer. It is a process based on the Customer Identification Program mandated by the Patriot Act of 2001. It has enhanced due diligence programs to address money laundering and the financing of terrorism in addition to financial fraud.

17-2. Background check

17-3. Sales and underwriting

17-4. True

17-5. Acceptable, restricted, prohibited

17-6. To limit the financial risks to the ISO, businesses and their ownership must be checked for bankruptcies, tax liens, criminal activity, financial judgments, and MATCH.

17-7. There is less risk for business owners where the cardholder is present with the card.

17-8. The MCC/SIC is the code that identifies an industry type. Analyzing an industry average against a specific company can help to pinpoint issues with Chargebacks or Retrievals in time to prevent heavy fraud losses either by placing reserves on certain industry types or declining them altogether.

17-9. Determining companies that fall under restricted or prohibited categories where the risk of fraud and Chargebacks is much higher, including adult, online, tobacco, etc.

17-10. There is the possibility that the agent intentionally altered the MCC/SIC to hide the true nature of the business and that underwriting failed to verify the true nature of the business.

17-11.
- Charged as an accessory to a crime
- Exposure to heavy losses from Chargebacks
- Loss of sponsorship from the acquiring bank and processor

17-12. False. Reserves are to protect ISOs from merchants who are expected to have high occurrence of Chargebacks.

18-1. Why do you need to define your purpose?

18-2. What should the developer ask about first?

18-3. True or False: Business owners are advised to do business with an insured company with insurance rather than individual who does not carry such insurance.

18-4. Is this chapter intended for merchants planning sales sites or agents and ISOs planning business sites? Should you have options regarding maintenance and support?

18-6. True or False: It is always prohibited for ISOs and agents to use images of the card brands on their websites.

ANSWERS

18-1. To deliver the best results the first time

18-2. The outcomes and purpose of the website

18-3. True

18-4. Both. Agents are also advised to work with web developers as a referral source as a developer will need a resource for his clients.

18-5. True.

18-6. False. Although many ISO trainers will disagree, there is one circumstance in which an ISO or agent is allowed to use the service marks, and in which he or she would be *required* to use them. That way, of course, is for the ISO or agent to accept credit cards. Just as merchants are required to show the marks on their doors or websites, the ISO would be required to do so. If you wish to list service marks on your website, you will need to accept credit cards for equipment and setup fees.

CHAPTER 19
ASSOCIATIONS

19-1. What organization did the Bankcard Services Association (BSA) become?

19-2. True or False: What became the Northeast Acquirers' Association began before the BSA.

19-3. What organization entering the group prompted the name to change to the Northeast Acquirers' Association in 1997?

19-4. Which group also came to the NEAA winter conference in 1997?

19-5. In 1999; John McCormick, Judy Foster, and Audrey Blackmon formed the _____ _____.

19-6. The first Midwest Acquirers' Association conference was held in July of what year?

19-7. What industry trainer has well attended seminars at the association conferences?

19-8. What association conferences are available to the MLS or ISOs?

19-9. What are some reasons to attend regional conferences?

Activity

Select one regional conference to attend this year.

Discussion Topics/Notes

ANSWERS

19-1. The Electronic Transactions Association (ETA)

19-2. True. What became the NEAA began in 1985 while the BSA began in 1990.

19-3. American Express

19-4. The Merchant Level Salesperson (MLS)

19-5. Southeastern Acquirers' Association (SEAA). The first SEAA conference came 18 months later.

19-6. 2003

19-7. Mark Dunn's Field Guide Seminar

19-8.
- NEAA Winter Conference
- SEAA Conference
- ETA Conference (entry fees are typically higher)
- MWAA Conference
- WSAA Conference

19-9.
- Meeting your ISO's personnel
- Evaluating competition
- Evaluating terminals and value-added products
- Meeting other agents

20-1. What are Beauchamp's four steps to developing leads?

For the following questions, use Figure 20-1 on page 245 of the book.

20-2. Where does Beauchamp get the $710 for the 12 month annual profit?

20-3. What is the number of sales needed to hit the annual goal?

20-4. Why are monthly sales numbers not included in this calculation?

20-5. What is the purpose of the chart/figure?

20-6. List the five personal variables for this chart.

20-7. List the six questions that will help you clarify your prospecting strategy.

20-8. Which prospecting tactics listed on pp. 247–248 are the best ones to use?

20-9. If you need to call 50 people in a day to make three solid appointments, when do you call it a day?
    A. After you get three solid appointments
    B. After you have made 50 calls
    C. After you have worked a full day
    D. After you have three or more solid appointments and at least 50 calls

20-10. Remember, massive action yields massive _____.

Activities

1. Select five tactics. Plan and implement their use and track the results.

2. Create a prospecting list. Can any of these become a specialty industry for you (a vertical)?

3. Explore your options by entering your numbers in the boxes below and continue to refine them as your techniques improve. (Refer to Figure 20-1 on p. 245.)

Contact Requirement Worksheet				
Yearly income goal				
Average commission per sale (This will vary based on merchant type and commission structure. It includes income such as terminal sale, application bonus, or lease commission.)				
Annual residual value of the merchant (This will vary based upon merchant type, cost structure, and discount rate sold. Example is based on $30/month residual $\times$ 12 months.)				
12-month average profit per sale (Add the average commission per sale to the annual residual value of the merchant.)				
Number of sales required to meet the yearly income goal (Divide the income goal by the 12-month average profit per sale.)				
Weekly number of sales required to meet the income goal (There are 49 working weeks per year. Divide the yearly sales by 49.)				
Closing ratio per presentation (This will improve as sales skills improve. If not known, use 20% to be safe.)				
Number of sales presentations required per week (Divide the weekly sales goal by the closing ratio.)				
Appointment ratio (This is the number of prospect contacts made to deliver one sales presentation. If not known, use 10% as an example.)				
Total number of weekly prospect contacts required to meet presentation goal (Divide weekly presentations by appointment ratio percentage.)				
Daily number of contacts required (Divide total weekly prospect contacts by 5 workdays.)				

Discussion Topics/Notes

ANSWERS

20-1.
1. Determining contact requirement
2. Developing a prospecting strategy
3. Choosing the right prospecting tactics
4. Taking massive action

20-2. By combining the $350 average commission per sale and the $360 annual residual value

20-3. 106. (Some editions wrongly stated $106 Sales/month.)

20-4. Because Beauchamp recommends using a 49-week year to account for vacations and a monthly calculation would be skewed.

20-5. To allow agents to calculate exactly how many contacts a day are needed to hit his goals based on his production averages.

20-6.
1. Annual income goal
2. Average commission per sale
3. Annual residual value
4. Closing ratio per presentation
5. Appointment/presentation ratio per contact

20-7.
1. Who is my ideal prospect?
2. Where do I find my prospect?
3. What does my prospect want?
4. Why should they buy from me?
5. How do I penetrate this market?
6. When is my launch date?

20-8. All 23 of the methods listed are successful for some agents. It will be your job to try different ones and measure the effectiveness of each.

20-9. D. After you have three or more solid appointments and at least 50 calls

The most successful agents will continue calling after getting the goal of three solid appointments until the 50 calls are made. Once the production goals are met, continue working on other tasks.

20-10. Results

21-1. What two things can an MLS do with LinkedIn to help himself?

21-2. According to Caruso, what is LinkedIn's best kept secret?

21-3. How can agents make this work for them?

21-4. How can an agent use blogs?

21-5. If you discover that your prospect uses Infusionsoft for her shopping cart and system, what information does that give the smart sales agent?

Complete as many topics as you believe apply to you and track to see the ROI on your time.

Why is this chapter in the book? It gives basics from a renowned expert on social media. Some tips apply well to agents and it gives valuable advice that merchants pay Caruso to receive.

ANSWERS

21-1.
1. Find and join groups concerned with credit card processing to learn or share knowledge.
2. Research industries or prospects.

21-2. The recommendations feature

21-3. Ask your clients for recommendations. Be prepared to give them recommendations first.

21-4. List weekly tips on processing and build your reputation locally. You can also build goodwill with clients by mentioning them.

21-5. *Do not* sell on price. The merchant is paying up to $999 per month for Infusion-soft. Sell on the quality of your service and build some profit into the account. Selling on price may actually drive this client away as the perception is low price, low quality.

22-1. Jay Conrad Levinson said, "Marketing is everything you do to promote your business from the first point of _____ to the point at which _____ your business on a regular term."

22-2. In the section on developing a marketing mindset, what important reminder was inserted into the chapter for MLS and non-registered ISOs?

22-3. Focus your marketing on your _____, not your _____.

22-4. True or False: Barris recommends picking one strategy and sticking to it.

22-5. Track the response to your marketing so you can _____ of what is working and _____ what do not.

22-6. How does this chapter compare with Chapter 20 on Prospecting?

ANSWERS

22-1. Conception, customers patronize

22-2. Follow the rules of the card brands concerning marketing. That is, do not market under your own name unless you are registered with the card brands.

22-3. Potential clients, company

22-4. False. He recommends using a variety of ways.

22-5. Do more of, eliminate

22-6. This chapter is written for general business owners and Chapter 20 applies some of the concepts to an agent-specific audience.

23-1.   Name six common networking goals.

23-2.   What should your search include for a group?

23-3.   True or False: The best group is the one that gives you the most leads with the least amount of work.

23-4.   The number of referrals you _____ will determine the number of leads you will receive. If you cannot give referrals, you _____.

23-5.   The most important element of any referral-based networking group is its _____ _____.

23-6.   True or False: The best networking and referral generation meetings are professionally run, not social events.

23-7. What is the reason for category exclusivity?

23-8. What can happen if you provide training in a referral group?

23-9. Ultimately, who is responsible for your success in a referral group?

23-10. Why does Gifford believe cross-chapter networking is a critical benefit?

Discussion Topics/Notes

23-1.
1. Institutional advertising or creating brand awareness
2. Sales and marketing
3. Referral and strategic partners
4. Resource development
5. Mastermind group development
6. Career advancement

23-2.
- Clearly identify your goals.
- Define the geography that you want to work.
- Preliminarily select two or three groups that serve that geographical area.
- Research the offerings of each group.
- Visit and evaluate the specific group or chapter.
- Select, participate, and evaluate your results.

23-3. False. Some groups may give leads faster than others, but if you fail to give back legitimate leads, the leads you receive will dry up.

23-4. Give, will fail

23-5. Membership

23-6. True

23-7. To protect a member's business and referral stream. If you are the group's credit card processing member, then no other processor can come to your group meetings and discuss your category.

23-8. Double, triple, or quadruple the amount of referrals that members receive.

23-9. You are responsible for either your success or your failure. Personal accountability is critical.

23-10. It encourages you, as a member, to visit other groups that do not have a member in the category that you represent. It allows you to meet more members and get more exposure.

CHAPTER 24

INDENTIFYING REFERRAL AND STRATEGIC PARTNERS

24-1. What is a referral partner?

24-2. Define "strategic partner."

24-3. Why are referral partners so effective?

24-4. When you call on a prospect that has been referred, you are viewed as a _____, not a salesperson.

24-5. For what reason should the MLS be interested in referral partners?

24.6.   What are the five essential ingredients for an effective referral partner relationship?

24-7.   True or False: Anyone can be a referral partner.

24-8.   True or False: Even the best referral partners need to be trained to be effective.

24-9.   Referral partner relationships can ultimately save you _____, and can result in a _____, and _____.

24-10. What are two ways to destroy a referral partner relationship?

Discussion Topics/Notes

ANSWERS

24-1. A referral partner is an individual who agrees to generate referrals for you in return for your assistance in generating referrals for him.

24-2. A strategic partner offers products or services that are complementary to your own, or that markets to individuals who are also within your target market.

24-3.
- A referral partner is marketing you to people they know.
- He is viewed as a friend, not a salesperson.

24-4. Problem solver

24-5. Price is less of an issue and the prospect is more likely to accept recommended products and services.

24.6.
1. Trust
2. Commitment
3. Ability to generate referrals
4. Knowledge of each other's businesses
5. Taking action

24-7. False. Very few people deserve to be your referral partner.

24-8. True

24-9. Time, higher closing ratio, larger average sales

24-10.
1. Fail to call a referral promptly
2. Do not take care of a referral

25-1. True or False: To keep your pipeline full, you need to attend networking events regularly, not just when you are slow.

25-2. True or False: You should expect to make sales at a networking event.

25-3. At a networking event, be willing to meet _____ and _____. Do not _____ based on appearances.

25-4. What activity is crucial to perform within 48 hours after any networking event?

25-5. What six details does LaDouceur recommend you write on the back of a business card when you meet someone?

25-6. LaDouceur recommends which method of tracking contacts from events?
   A. Using rubber bands to bind business cards from each event
   B. Using a notebook planner to record activities
   C. Use a contact database program
   D. Using a tape recorder

ANSWERS

25-1. True

25-2. False. You are there to create relationships. Trying to sell people will turn them off.

25-3. Anyone, everyone, judge

25-4. Follow up

25-5.
    1. The date
    2. The name of the event
    3. Next action step for this prospect
    4. Deadline for this step
    5. First impressions
    6. Special details

25-6.C. Use a contact database program

26-1. Sparr believes that _____ out of every 100 calls will result in a new client while cold calling on the phone.

26-2. Pick a _____ in which you want to work.

26-3. Why does Sparr recommend a specific target market or vertical?
  A. To become an industry specialist
  B. To build a client base
  C. To build a higher residual
  D. All of the above

26-4. Why are referral partners recommended?

26-5. What is the best compensation for referral partners?

26-6. Can you just start out from day one with referral partners?

26-7. The conversion rate starting out with referral partners is _____, which is _____ times higher than the cold calling conversion rate.

26-8. What does Sparr suggest doing to get to know your partners better?

26-9. It usually takes _____ to get a group running well.

26-10. How many groups of referral partners can you have?

Discussion Topics/Notes

ANSWERS

26-1.   Two

26-2   Specific target market (vertical)

26-3.   D. All of the above

26-4.   Referral partners already have a customer base in the field you are seeking. Establishing partnerships with non-competitors seeking the same market you are can save a lot of time and effort.

26-5.   Referrals to your clients

26-6.   No. You will have no clients to return referrals. You need to build up a client base through other methods including cold calling.

26-7.   Two in ten, ten

26-8.   One day each week go out with your partners on sales calls.

26-9.   A year or so

26-10. As many as you can properly support. Take a year building the first one then add others and build using what you have learned.

27-1. True or False: Tracy believes that everyone is in the business of selling.

27-2. Dwight D. Eisenhower once said, "The art of leadership is getting people to do what you want them to do and _____."

27-3. The ability to persuade and influence others is central to _____.

27-4. What is the Pareto Principle and how does it affect you as a salesperson?

27-5. What three factors are essential in sales, wherein all three must be properly suited to one another?

27-6. True or False: It is hard, if not impossible, for a sales agent to sell a product or service that he does not believe in and cannot commit to wholeheartedly.

27-7. Nothing happens until a _____ takes place.

27-8. What does Tracy mean when he says, "No matter how good a product or service may be, in a competitive market and with customers who are busy and preoccupied with many other things, products and services must ultimately be sold."

27-9. The ability to get the customer to _____ is vital to the entire sales process.

27-10. _____ of sales are closed only after the _____ closing attempt.

27-11. What percent of salespeople fail to ask, even one time, for the sale?

27-12. Top salespeople see _____ and ask _____.

27-13. Your own personal level of _____ and _____ more often determines your sales and income than any other factor.

27-14. What is the single most important factor in achieving high sales goals?

27-15. If your income goal is $75,000, what is each working hour worth according to Tracy's method of calculation?

27-16. Sales success comes from fulfilling _____, not _____.

27-17. Every product or service can be viewed as the _____ to a problem.

27-18. The more pressing the problem or need is for you to solve, the less _____ _____ the client will be.

27-19. Testimonials of any kind will increase _____ and lower _____ _____ to a product or service.

27-20. How does Tracy recommend building trust with a prospect?
    A. Saying "trust me"
    B. Asking about the prospect's life and sports teams
    C. Asking penetrating questions that identify a prospect's needs
    D. None of the above

27-21. Define the 70/30 rule that top salespeople use.

27-22. The way that you are viewed by your prospects determines your _____.

27-23. The best salespeople _____ before each call.

27-24. *How to Win Customers* author Heinz Goldman says that _____ of salespeople could improve their results by rewording their presentations.

Follow the chapter instructions on applying the laws of selling.

ANSWERS

27-1. True. "All of us are paid both tangibly and intangibly, on the basis of how well we sell ourselves, our ideas, and our products and services to others. It is not a matter of whether you sell or not, it is only a matter of how good you are at it."

27-2. To think of it as their own idea

27-3. A happy life

27-4. The 80/20 rule. The top 20 percent make 80% of the sales and 80 percent of the money. Research shows the top 10 percent of sales people open 80% of the new accounts and are some of the highest paid people in the world.

27-5.
1. The product or service
2. The sales person
3. The customer

27-6. True. This means that people who are not successful in this industry may still be great salespeople in another line of sales. Also, just because one was successful in another line of sales, does not mean he will be successful in merchant sales.

27-7. Sale

27-8. He means that very few merchants will seek you out. It is up to you to get in front of the merchant and show why you deserve his business. Some ISO trainers will take this one step further and remind agents that since they will not have merchants coming to them, they should not be selling on price.

27-9.　Take action

27-10.　80%, fifth. Set up a conversation to ask for the order in different ways.

27-11.　50%, half of salespeople fail to ask for the sale

27-12.　More people, more often

27-13.　Desire, ambition

27-14.　Setting them

27-15.　$37.50

27-16.　Existing needs, not creating new ones

27-17.　Solution. One benefit of developing a niche or specialty is that once you understand the problems faced, your solutions can be offered to others in the industry.

27-18.　Price sensitive

27-19.　Desirability, price resistance

27-20.　C. Asking penetrating questions that identify the prospect's needs.

27-21.　Listen 70% of the time.

27-22.　Income

27-23.　Prepare thoroughly

27-24.　95%

CHAPTER 28
COLD CALLING

28-1. List a few reasons why cold calling is unpopular with salespeople.

28-2. Most attempts at cold calling are going to be _____.

28-3. True or False: With proper preparation, you can achieve a success rate consistently over 20%.

28-4. What major and unique advantage does cold calling give that other forms of marketing do not?

28-5. Think of cold calling the way the army thinks of a _____.

28-6. List five benefits of cold calling.

28-7. True or False: Grimer states that you need to call the decision maker, not go higher or lower in ranking.

28-8. How is the advice given by Grimer applicable to the MLS?

28-9. What topics are best to use in your value proposition?

28-10. The most important aspect of a cold call is to make clear to the person you are calling how your product or service benefits him in the _____.

28-11. Approximately how many words should comprise your opening statement?

28-12. Which is an appropriate use of a cold call?
   A. To gather information on a prospect's needs
   B. To set up an appointment
   C. To close the sale
   D. All of the above
   E. None of the above

28-13. What suggestion does Grimer make about salespeople?

28-14. What times are recommended for cold calling and why?

28-15. True or False: Grimer recommends that you always leave a voicemail message.

Activity

Review and take action on Grimer's Ten-Point Plan.

Discussion Topics/Notes

28-1.
- It is hard work
- Psychologically challenging
- Requires attention to detail, concentration, tenacity, and preparation
- Rejection

28-2. Failures

28-3. True

28-4. A guarantee of a response of some sort

28-5. Sniper

28-6.
1. Collect feedback
2. Fine control of pipeline
3. A more complete and up-to-date understanding of where your competitors are succeeding and failing
4. Long-term relationship building
5. Exact targeting

28-7. True

28-8. The MLS should target the decision maker if known. If unknown, always aim for the owner since he is most often the decision maker.

28-9.
- Profitability—does it help the owner make more money?
- Cost cutting
- Legal protection (perhaps a lead-in with PCI)
- Reputation

28-10. Opening 20 seconds

28-11. No more than 60-80

28-12. D. All of the above

For an MLS, all are appropriate with single store owners.

28-13. If leads/appointments are set up by others, reduce the salesperson's commission.

28-14. 7 a.m.–8:30 a.m. and 5:30 p.m.–7 p.m., to avoid the gatekeepers and get directly through.

28-15. False. A voicemail message can do more harm than good.

29-1. What are seven advantages of phone sales over regular sales calls?

29-2. What are the two types of phone sales?

29-3. What is the difference between Bruno's types and Grimer's and why is that?

29-4. Compare and contrast "all phone sales" from "appointment calls."

29-5. What items comprise Bruno's checklist that should be ready before picking up the phone?

29-6. Why is a target market important?

29-7. What is the purpose of a sales script?

29-8. What is the basic outline for a sales call?

29-9. True or False: "All sales" calls consist of cold calling each day.

29-10. Name the items to keep in mind while making your calls.

Discussion Topics/Notes

ANSWERS

29-1.

1. You can call anywhere in the country.
2. You can call more businesses in a day than you can visit.
3. More calls mean more clients.
4. You can save gas.
5. You can save time.
6. You can do it at home or at an office away from the elements (rain, snow, heat).
7. Isolated events have less influence on residuals.

29-2.

1. Appointment setting
2. Sales

29-3. Grimer is an expert at calling CEOs of larger companies. There is normally little need in merchant processing sales for an information gathering call.

29-4. The goal in "all phone sales" is to show the decision-maker that you can completely provide all of the services needed without ever stepping foot on site. Your job is to get merchants to fax you the statements and completed applications.

"Appointment calls" are targeted to local area businesses where a representative will finish the sales process in person. Depending on the set up, the statements may be faxed in for analysis before the appointment or will be made available at the appointment.

29-5.

- Target industry
- Common equipment used in the industry
- Known issues or concerns for industry
- Knowing how your products can solve these problems
- Known potential objections

29-6. Calling across the country allows you to specialize on one industry. This is an advantage as you learn the industry and become familiar with its processes, equipment needed, and common objections for which you can prepare.

29-7. Maintain consistency and cover the pitch completely. Shooting from the hip or a random approach can cause you to lose your train of thought or not cover key areas of the presentation.

29-8.
- Introduction
- Meet decision maker, qualify, and clarify
- Identify problems
- Box and start closing
- Identify solutions
- Close

29-9. False. Matt recommends two days devoted to cold calls, two to follow-ups, and a wild card.

29-10.
- Stay on topic by using your script
- Monitor your successes (take breaks every 10 or 20 calls)
- Always set follow-up calls
- Always be polite
- Know when to end a conversation

30-1. In the opinion of Waters, if you are not speaking to a decision-maker, who are you speaking to?

30-2. True or False: A gatekeeper can be an excellent ally or a mighty foe.

30-3. How does Waters define the stages of a cold call?

30-4. True or False: Tell the gatekeeper what you have to offer.

30-5. Why should saying, "Hi, this is Tom. Is the owner around?" or asking for the owner by his first name alone help you to get around the gatekeeper?

30-6. What does Waters suggest if the gatekeeper hangs up on you?

30-7. Why is the Internet your friend?

30-8. What kind of information can gatekeepers provide?

30-9. What is recommended for every cold call whether in person or by phone?

30-10. What is the major difference between this chapter and Greg Grimer's chapter on cold calling?

30-11. What is the reason for the difference?

30-12. How do you personally feel about implying that your call is normal and welcome?

Discussion Topics/Notes

30-1. A gatekeeper

30-2. True

30-3.
1. Identify a potential prospect
2. Identify decision maker
3. Work with or through the gatekeepers
4. Reach the decision maker
5. Making the sale

30-4. False. Never solicit the gatekeeper.

30-5. By being vague and using a relaxed tone, you may convince the gatekeeper that you know the business owner personally.

30-6. Call back and suggest that you were cut off.

30-7.
- Search for address
- See picture of the business
- Find the owner's name
- Search for corporate profiles

30-8.
- Current equipment
- Current processes (keying into terminal or virtual terminal)
- Volume to determine if it is worth your time
- Issues with current processor

30-9.
- Take good notes after each call.
- Ask "Who is the person that handles your merchant account?" and "How do I reach him?"

30-10. Grimer's chapter discourages trying to get through the gatekeepers while Waters believes that it is not only possible to get through them but to engage them in the process.

30-11. Grimer's experience is with larger companies and professional gatekeepers (executive secretaries or executive assistants). Waters defines everyone who is not a decision-maker to be a gatekeeper. These gatekeepers may hold valuable information that can help. Also, the companies that most MLS will contact will typically be small single location stores.

31-1. Who does a thin pricing model benefit?

31-2. Can the honest MLS compete against the thin pricing model?

31-3. Why does Holman recommend pursuing a single type of business (niche)?

31-4. Define the KISS technique and how it is used.

31-5. What is the worst thing you can do while interviewing a business owner and why?

31-6. Why do you want to recap what a merchant shared with you?

31-7. How should you finish the interview?

31-8. Do not be afraid to...?

31-9. What two fees does Dave tend to sell against?

31-10. Do not formulate your next question while _____.

31-11. Besides advising a client on how to run his business, what is the worst thing an agent can do?

31-12. Define ABC.

31-13. Why does Holman recommend that agents have their picture on business cards?

31-14. Why does Holman refer to his customers/merchants as clients?

Discussion Topics/Notes

ANSWERS

31-1. Only the processor. At 20 basis points, only $20 is generated on sales of $10,000 and that is before the split with the ISO/processor. The 10 bp split yields $20,000 on a portfolio of $10,000,000.

31-2. Yes

31-3. So you can specialize and learn in detail a business that you have an interest in.

31-4. Keep it simple, stupid. Ask questions without giving advice.

31-5. Tell a merchant how to run his business. The business owner works in his business, you do not. It comes across as arrogant and offensive to be instructed by someone with no experience in the line of business.

31-6. To show that you were listening and to confirm her concerns

31-7. A qualifying question, asking if anything was left out or if there is anything else that the merchant would like to share

31-8. Tell her what she does not need or what you honestly feel is not in her best interest

31-9. Monthly paper supply fees and PCI fees

31-10. The prospect is still answering your previous question

31-11. Discuss solutions for the prospect before asking him what his problems are. If you walk in talking about what you want to sell, you will lose the opportunity to sell what the prospect needs.

31-12. Always Be Closing

31-13. When you return at a later time, there is a sense of familiarity and the perception that the prospect knows you.

31-14. To project a professional approach similar to an accountant or attorney

32-1. True or False: Completing an application properly is a critical part of the selling process.

32-2. Why are the funds deposited in a merchant's account for card processing considered a loan?

32-3. True or False: If you have a reason to suspect fraud might occur, you do not have to say anything that might cause the application to be held or rejected.

32-4. Underwriting a merchant processing application is similar to the process of what? Why do you think that is?

32-5. What example does Fortney use as a low-risk merchant and why?

32-6. What is Fortney's example of higher risk?

32-7. Why does Fortney suggest the preamble at the top of page 420?

32-8. True or False: It is better to ask about the merchant's concerns before you begin completing the application rather than during its completion.

32-9. Knowing a merchant well often leads to _____.

32-10. The underwriter will only _____.

32-11. What will happen if the sales agent loses control of the process of completing the application?

32-12. Why are two signatures typically required on a processing contract?

32-13. What is the difference between the signature lines and why is it required?

32-14. Getting an accurate tax identification is important. Name a tip to get an accurate TIN and why it works well (not in the book).

32-15. Can a sales agent waive the requirement for getting the Social Security Number of the owner or officer signing the guarantee?

32-16. What will happen if volume, average ticket, or high ticket amounts listed on application are too low?

32-17. What are the two best sources for finding accurate numbers for the application?

32-18. From the processor's perspective, why is the site survey critical to the application process?

32-19. Name a few items on the site survey.

32-20. What are the risks to an agent who knowingly makes a false statement on the site survey?

32-21. What is listed in the equipment section of the application?

32-22. True or False: When completing the pricing section of the contract, the MLS only needs to know whether Interchange Plus (IC+) or Tiered Pricing is pertinent.

32-23. When should a sales agent be fully aware of her pricing options?

1. What is the best way to price an account?

One suggestion is using your Schedule A to determine a profitable margin on each price point used and to set enough of a profit to keep you comfortably in business. If you cannot create an income, you will not be able to remain in the business.

2. What are some suggestions from your ISO on how to minimize merchant fraud and produce clean applications?

ANSWERS

32-1.   True. Mistakes can result in a rejected application and some prospects will not re-sign the corrected application.

32-2.   Because the customer and issuing bank still have a right to reverse the transaction

32-3.   False. The sales agent has a duty to report his suspicions to the underwriters and the ISO or processor. Failure to do so can result in loss of the residual, either through the contractual language or should the partner go under as a result of losses.

32-4.   The method that banks use in analyzing loan applications. Since consumers and issuing banks can initiate Chargebacks, processors need to be confident that the merchant will be around to satisfy the client/issuer.

32-5.   Restaurants that do not cater. Since the meal is delivered before payment is rendered, there is low risk for Chargebacks.

32-6.   A furniture store with higher tickets that provides delivery at a future date. Delays can lead to Chargebacks.

32-7.   To put the merchant at ease about why you are requesting the information for the application. It will create less strain during completion of the application.

32-8.   True

32-9.   Failure to disclose data

32-10. See what is given to them and likely not make assumptions.

32-11. He will omit crucial information and need to return to the client, risking loss of the contract or damage to his reputation.

32-12. One signature is to accept the contract on behalf of the company and the other is a personal guarantee.

32-13. One line has the title of the signer and the other excludes a title. This is required because a title is not included with a personal guarantee because it is separate from the obligation of the company.

32-14. Include a W-9 in your application paperwork. This works well because the merchant sees this as an IRS form that carries a penalty if the wrong number is used.

32-15. No. But with the processor's authorization, nonprofits and some corporations may be allowed to have no personal guarantee. Be advised, however, this may lengthen the underwriting process and will likely require the merchant's financial reports including tax returns and balance sheets.

32-16. The processor will not account for the higher numbers in underwriting and will likely place holds on the funds, which may cost the agent the account.

32-17.
1. Previous statements
2. Asking the merchant for numbers and cycles unseen on statements

32-18. The site survey allows the sales agent to be the eyes and ears of the underwriter who relies on its honest completion to properly gauge the risk to the processor.

32-19.
- Was the survey done in person or by phone?
- Is the location owned or leased?
- Landlord's name and phone
- Square footage
- Type of building (storefront, office, residential)
- Pictures
- Suppliers
- Does the merchant have sufficient supply to meet demand?
- Is the company actively in business today? When is it opening?
- What is the time between sale and delivery?
- Does the seller ship or is a third party responsible?

32-20.
- Possible responsibility for merchant fraud
- Lost revenue from the merchant
- Termination of the contract and loss of all residuals for fraud
- Possible criminal charges for fraud

32-21. The current equipment if you will be reprogramming it. Special features like auto batching can be included here as well as instructions for staging when you will be using a gateway like ePN.

32-22. False. The sales agent needs to understand how the processor prices the accounts so that he is in sync with it.

If the processor uses a surcharge method and fills in the application with the specific rates of 1.74%, 2.59% for MQ, and 3.29% for NQ, the merchant will find MQ rates of 4.33% and NQ rates of 5.03%. Whereas, if the processor expects full rates and you list only surcharges, you will under-price the merchant.

32-23. Before completing the pricing page, better yet before visiting a merchant.

33-1. Give at least four definitions of customer service.

33-2. Who sets the expectations for customer service?

33-3. Who is typically the first one called when the merchant has an issue?

33-4. In what ways is a merchant "touched?"

33-5. How does Mathews define good customer service?

33-6. What are the customer service metrics noted by the National Business Research Institute?

33-7. What did Visa's Merchant Functional Cost Study report as the annual merchant servicing expense per 1,000 MIDs a decade ago?

33-8. What expenses make up the customer service cost for the MLS?

33-9. On a medium-sized portfolio for an ISO, what items make up the investment for customer service?

33-10. Why should an ISO spend so much on customer service?

33-11. True or False: An agent should share the results of customer surveys and press clippings.

33-12. What five items are tantamount to professionally providing customer service?

Discussion Topics/Notes

33-1.

1. "The ability to provide a service or product as promised."
2. "About treating others as you would like them to treat you."
3. "An organization's ability to supply its customers' wants and needs."
4. "The process of taking care of customers in a positive manner."
5. "Any contact between a customer and a company, which causes a negative or positive perception by a customer."
6. "A process for providing competitive advantage and adding benefits that maximize the total value to the customer."
7. "The commitment to providing value-added services to external and internal customers, including attitude, knowledge, technical support, and quality of service in a timely manner."
8. "A proactive attitude that we may sum up as: I care and I can do."

33-2. The sales agent sets the expectation during the sales process.

33-3. The sales agent that he signed with.

33-4.

- Contract
- Lease or rental agreements
- Initial training
- Equipment configuration
- Kitting and deployment
- Hardware and software issues
- Answering questions
- Deposits
- Upgrades to equipment

33-5. Good customer service is satisfying your merchant in a timely and cost-effective manner that enhances your value to the merchant. Poor customer service is any action that differs from that simple statement.

33-6.

- Quality of service
- Speed of service
- Pricing
- Complaints or problems
- Trust in your employees
- Closeness of the relationship with contacts in your firm
- Types of other services needed

33-7. $3,508 for large programs and $1,400 for small programs

33-8. The phone, a light CRM package, car expenses, and time away from selling

33-9.
- Sophisticated multi-line telephone system
- Computer system and IT support
- Complex CRM systems
- Overhead
- Management
- Customer service staff
- Loyalty and retention bonuses

33-10. It costs more to gain new customers than to retain current customers.

33-11. True. Mathews says just be sure the results are where you want them to be.

33-12.
1. Attitude
2. Honesty
3. Forthrightness
4. Thoroughness
5. Accuracy

34-1. What are the four main ways of placing a terminal?

34-2. What does Pirtle advise MLS and ISOs do before offering "Free" equipment?

34-3. Who determines just how good the HarborTouch free POS program is?

34-4. True or False: It is more ethical and respectable to sell terminals than to give free use or lease them.

34-5. When setting up your own merchant account, what rate should you set it at and why?

34-6. How do you determine your payout on a lease?

34-7. The payout for the lease minus _____ is your commission for the lease.

34-8. What percentage of the annual lease payment is subtracted from the merchant's taxes due?
   A. 25%
   B. 30%
   C. 36%
   D. 100%
   E. It depends upon the tax bracket of the merchant.

34-9. What determines whether a terminal is free, sold, or leased?

Activities

1. Practice configuring the lease factors, terms, and dollar amounts to get used to calculating.

2. Investigate different prices on terminals to determine your commissions.

3. Research leasing companies and compare leasing factors.

Discussion Topics/Notes

34-1.
1. "Free"
2. Sell
3. Lease
4. Rent (hybrid of sales and leasing)

34-2. Check his Schedule A to determine whether it will affect his residual split or signing bonus.

34-3. HarborTouch, its agents, and its merchants using the program

34-4. False. All four options can be ethical and respectable. It is more about how the salesperson gets the contract signed.

34-5. Set your rate at your preferred rate for your merchants. If you want to charge IC+ 0.50% + $0.10 with a $10 statement fee and other fees; then charge them to yourself. Merchants will assume that as a salesperson in the industry, you have access to great pricing. Having a statement that talks about the fees you pay can convince merchants that the fees are reasonable. Depending on the split with your processor, you will get at least half the profit back in commission. Just don't be greedy.

34-6. Divide the monthly payment you set by the lease factor, which is determined by the client's credit rating.

34-7. Terminal cost

34-8. E. It depends upon the tax bracket of the merchant.

This question throws off most people because the amount paid is 100% deductible. The amount deducted from the tax amount is the pay out multiplied by the merchant's tax rate. The $600 in lease payments will be a $150 deduction at 25% and $180 at 30%. The deduction always involves the rate; a tax credit is a complete write off.

34-9. The needs of the merchant coupled with the profit desired and the perceived ethics and values of the salesperson. For example, a fleet may require leased mobile units and a store wanting six POS systems will be more comfortable leasing than spending up to $20,000 in capital it might need elsewhere. If an agent does not offer a leasing option because of a perceived ethics or values issue, he may lose the sale.

35-1. Define MTM and RTO and compare the options.

35-2. Does an MLS need a lot of capital to offer RTO?

35-3. What options does an MLS have with RTO?

35-4. True or False: RTO and MTM are morally superior to leasing.

35-5. Why does Tichelkamp believe merchants would be so willing to accept an RTO for $39/month instead of just buying it outright for $399?

35-6. Using Tichelkamp's projection of lease funding versus the total collected, what is the advantage to the agent of RTO versus selling the lease?

35-7. What are the disadvantages of RTO to the selling agent?

35-8. Calculate the approximate lease factor to obtain a payout of $1,484 for a $49 monthly payment.

35-9. Why is it important to know how to calculate the lease factor?

35-10. What services can you include in a MTM or RTO setup?

35-11. What are two ways of protecting your equipment and account?

35-12. How can you take the payments?

Discussion Topics/Notes

Does your ISO allow for independently charging a merchant for any reason?

ANSWERS

35-1. MTM is renting month-to-month. MTO is considered to be a pure profit endeavor. The merchant can pay five years or more and not own the terminal.

RTO is rent-to-own and will essentially allow a merchant to pay for a terminal over time, plus an additional amount. At the end of the term, he owns the terminal.

35-2. No. With RTO, you charge a down payment, which can either cover your cost or pay a good portion of it. If you do not fully cover cost, you can within a short time.

35-3. RTO is flexible. You can offer RTO instead of a lease and earn money over time, or set a short term for the merchant to spread out payment.

35-4. False. RTO, MTM, and leases are all morally acceptable options available to the MLS. It is not the option, but the methods used by the agent that will determine the morality of any contract.

35-5. Merchant sees an advantage to extending payments

35-6. Agent will make an additional $868 over the 4 years

35-7.
- It will take 4 years to make the money versus an immediate lease payout.
- Agent has responsibility for collection.
- The contract is cancellable for RTO or MTM.

35-8. X = Lease Factor
$49/X = 1,484$
$49 = 1,484X$
$1 = 1,484X/49$
$1 = 30.2857X$
$0.0330 = X$
The Lease Factor is approximately 0.0330.

To explain:
$49/0.0330 = 1484.8484$ where the extra .8484 is from rounding
$49/X = 1.484$
Using algebra. multiply both sides of equation by X to get $49 = 1,484X$
Divide both sides of equation by 49 to get $1 = 1,484X/49$
$1,484/49$ is approximately 30.2857 (rounded to four places)
You now have $1 = 30.2857X$
Divide both sides by 30.2857 to get $1/30.2857 = X$
$1/30.2857$ is 0.0330 (rounded to four places)
So $X = 0.0330$
$49/0.0330 = 1484.8484$

35-9.   Simply comparing payouts may not be enough to make your decision on when to offer a lease or RTO. Lease factors are tied to the merchant's credit score. In the Chapter 34 example, 0.330 falls between B and C credit. Since there is a risk to the MLS for self-placement, you need to consider the credit score and include that in the decision as to whether to offer a lease or RTO.

35-10. The MLS can roll gift cards, check services, or most other services into a MTM or RTO setup.

35-11.

- Have an attorney create a detailed contract listing the rights and obligations of both parties.
- Place a customized password on the terminal so no one else can download to it.

35-12.

- Your ISO can take them.
- You can ACH.
- You can accept checks.
- You can set up a recurring credit card payment.

36-1. Why does the MLS need to know about POS systems?

36-2. Why do POS providers typically specialize in one or two segments or niches?

36-3. Why did the POS vendors move in as competitors to the MLS?

36-4. What company did Cibley attribute for creating the marketing plan that UBC/ HarborTouch employed for its POS program?

36-5. What advantage does HarborTouch have over other ISOs and agents?

36-6. What is a potential issue with "free" POS systems?

36-7. Why is the POS system shown as "free" with quotation marks?

36-8. What was suggested for creative agents?

36-9. What are the basic avenues for ISOs to pursue if they want to enter the POS business?

36-10. What one item does Cibley attribute to the success of the small independent POS dealers?

36-11. List some of the business types that would be good referral partners for agents seeking restaurant POS accounts (Cibley refers to these as local vendors that you can refer to owners).

36-12. What three reasons do merchants give for choosing not to have a POS system?

36-13. List some ROI considerations that can help you sell a POS.

36-14. Name a few suggestions that Cibley gave to help POS merchants gain new customers.

Cibley's focus was on restaurants. For more information on POS systems in the gas station, liquor, and convenience markets, read Bill Scott's *Retail is Detail* (ISBN: 978-125782678-0, available on Amazon for $49.95) and acquaint yourself with his theory on UIIC (Unique Item Inventory Control) versus the more common category management. Bill owns a POS company that specializes in the retail side.

Discussion Topics/Notes

What POS system does your ISO recommend for your use and why?

36-1. So he can approach current high-volume merchants before a competitor does

36-2. So they can have the expertise required to understand the needs of merchants in that industry and anticipate questions

36-3. They saw the money that could be made in residuals.

36-4. Cibley believes that Gillette's giving away free razors to get the blade sales was the inspiration for HarborTouch.

36-5. HarborTouch trained its agents and ISOs in both card processing and POS sales.

36-6. While the "free" POS systems meet the basic needs for restaurateurs, there are many standard features absent. The ISO/agent needs to know that the system that he is offering meets the merchant's needs.

36-7. The systems are not truly free. There may be standard fees that the agent must charge to receive payments. The POS also has costs including monthly and quarterly service fees. Another issue is a 5-year commitment on credit card processing. It would be more accurate to describe the systems as having no upfront costs.

36-8. Find a POS partner and create a rent-to-own POS solution with gift cards and a service plan.

36-9.
1. Open a full dealership.
2. Align with a credit card processor that offers POS systems as part of its product line.
3. Develop a partnership with a local POS company that is not offering processing.

36-10. Having a 24/7 customer support system in place because restaurant owners are not very patient when they have a major problem closing out.

36-11.
- Restaurant broker
- Heating/AC/HVAC
- Used equipment broker
- Web designer
- Electrician
- Refrigeration
- Although not listed, plumbers and sewage companies can come in handy too

36-12.
1. He wants one but cannot afford the cost of a system.
2. He can afford one, but does not truly understand how a system will enhance his business and increase his bottom line.
3. He is convinced that a POS system will change the nature of his accounting system, which is based upon cash withdrawals.

36-13.
- Accuracy of checks
- Eliminates confusion on handwritten orders
- Servers remain on the floor
- Increasing table turns
- Miscellaneous cost savings like carbonless guest checks

36-14.
- Direct email programs like Constant Contact
- Integrated loyalty program
- Server contests
- Facebook, Twitter, Four Square, and other social media tools

37-1.   What are the two common wireless terminal networks?

37-2.   What is the enabler for mobile payments?

37-3.   List a few items that can be used to facilitate mobile payments.

37-4.   What are the benefits of mobile payments?

37-5.   According to credit reporting firm TransUnion, _____ of all card number thefts in a point-of-sale environment occur in _____.

37-6. _____ of consumers surveyed by research firm Moore & Symons are _____ when handing over their cards in table service restaurants.

37-7. What are some benefits to pay-at-the-table processing?

37-8. What is NFC?

37-9. What are the two benefits of contactless payments?

37-10. Market research firm Tower Group estimates that contactless payments can reduce individual transaction times by _____.

37-11. In the U.S., contactless payments up to _____ can be made without requiring cardholder authentication (i.e. signature).

37-12. Why is it desirable to establish a threshold for the amount at which a signature is required?

37-13. Is information safe when it is loaded into a phone's mobile wallet? Is NFC secure?

37-14. What can NFC be used for besides payments?

37-15. Which merchants should you target to sell NFC technology?

37-16. How does NFC work within a business?

37-17. Which phones are NFC ready?

37-18. A client runs an upscale restaurant. He does not like the idea of leaving the terminal at the table, or requiring customers to use the terminal at all. He prefers to have his wait staff complete the card transaction on behalf of the patron. Can he do this?

Activities

1. Using the list of industry magazines listed in Chapter 9, explore news concerning Mobile Wallets and list some of the companies developing the technology.

2. NFC saves both consumers and retailers time in processing card transactions. Compile a list of merchants in your area who have long lines and who do not accept contactless payments. From this list, find the industry most represented and learn its hot points by joining related associations or LinkedIn groups.

Discussion Topics/Notes

37-1.
1. General Packet Radio Service (GPRS)
2. Code Division Multiple Access (CDMA)

37-2. New technology

37-3.
- Droid smartphones
- iPhones
- iPads
- Mobile card devices

37-4.
- Completely portable payment acceptance solution
- Lower Interchange costs
- Fully encrypted card swipe prevents identity theft
- Fast network speeds for quick transaction processing
- Signature capture virtually eliminates merchant risk

37-5. 50%, restaurants

37-6. 60%, concerned about the safety of their account information

37-7.
- Protecting clients from identity theft
- Reducing the number of steps required to settle a check
- Increasing table turns
- Card never leaves the customer's sight
- All data encrypted at site
- Customer gets receipt quickly
- Increased table turns
- Increased customer satisfaction
- Improved profitability
- Higher tips for servers

37-8. Near-field communication is a technology that allows a card or a smartphone to establish communication with a device by touching or bringing it in close proximity.

37-9. Speed and convenience

37-10. 10-15 seconds

37-11. 50%

37-12. In busy retail environments, the speed of contactless transactions without signatures is attractive.

37-13. NFC-enabled credit and debit payment applications are secure. Personal information, including financial information such as an account number and expiration date, is stored in a secured area in the NFC phone, commonly called the "secure element."

37-14. NFC also can be used for loyalty programs. Your phone could keep track of points from the store and you could receive mobile coupons that you would be able to redeem with your phone.

37-15. Any merchant wanting to expand his options for payment acceptance. An offer of more ways to pay only increases customer satisfaction. Customer satisfaction equals more revenue for the merchant.

37-16. An NFC-enabled phone is equipped with a payment application and your payment account information (i.e., your credit or debit card). The application and payment account information are encrypted and stored in a secure area in the phone. The phone uses NFC technology to communicate with the merchant's contactless payment-capable POS system, similar to the contactless payment cards and devices in use today.

37-17. A list of phones is maintained and available at http://www.nfcworld.com/nfc-phones-list/

37-18. Yes. The wait staff can process the card like a traditional transaction using the terminal at the table and swiping the customer's card. The sales receipt has a blank tip line where the cardholder enters the tip. The cardholder will appreciate the added security of his card staying in his sight at the table, not to mention the speedier transaction.

38-1. By using a payment gateway, which type of merchant has the ability to transact electronically?

38-2. Payment gateway software can be used to process which types of payments?

38-3. Payment gateway software should meet the security standards as dictated by the PCI Council. What does PCI stand for?

38-4. By establishing an ecommerce account, the merchant has the ability to:
   A. Fulfill online orders
   B. Fulfill telephone orders
   C. Fulfill in-person orders
   D. Fulfill catalog orders
   E. A only
   F. All of the above

38-5. True or false: To facilitate an electronic transaction, a merchant must establish an Internet account with a service provider.

38-6. What is the definition of encryption?
   A. The activity of making clear or converting from code into plain text
   B. The process of transforming sensitive information into unreadable code
   C. The activity of hiding the expiration date and all but the last 4 digits of the credit card account number
   D. All of the above

38-7. As it pertains to encryption, what does SSL stand for?

38-8. What are the benefits of payment gateways to the merchant?
   A. Merchants can accept any type of electronic payment.
   B. Merchants can store customers' credit card data directly on their system for better customer service.
   C. Transactions are processed and authorized in real-time.
   D. Merchants can easily access transaction records for fast reconciliation.
   E. All of the above
   F. A, C, & D only

38-9. What are the key features that agents should look for when choosing to partner with a gateway provider?
   A. Accounts that are priced to make the agent the most in residual pay
   B. Software that is PA-DSS certified
   C. A gateway provider that also offers merchant processing to complement your product and fosters "friendly competition" between the two of you
   D. Online training tools that allow the processor to troubleshoot gateway issues directly, leaving the gateway provider out of the service cycle
   E. All of the above

1. Create a list of payments gateways and benefits to your merchants.

2. Explore which gateways do not compete with you for business. (In other words, which gateway providers do not offer processing to merchants?)

1. What gateway does your ISO recommend or require?

2. Does an agent have the option to use his own gateway?

ANSWERS

38-1.   Retail, mobile, and online

38-2.   Credit cards, debit cards, checks, and gift cards

38-3.   Payment card industry

38-4.   F. All of the above

38-5.   True

38-6.   B. The process of transforming sensitive information into unreadable code

38-7.   C. Secure socket layer

38-8.   F. A, C, & D only

38-9.   B. Software that is PA-DSS certified

39-1. True or False: The percentage of check payments processed electronically more than doubled from 2006 to 2009.

39-2. Name the technology invented in the 1950s that uses special ink toners and fonts to print account and routing information on checks.

39-3. What does ACH stand for?

39-4. _____ is the network created to more effectively process increasing volumes of checks by placing transaction data into electronic formats.

39-5. What organization is responsible for setting rules and guidelines governing ACH processing?

39-6. In what year did the Federal Reserve mandate that participants in the ACH network must deliver files electronically?

39-7. What is the name of the law that allowed for the use of a scanned image of a check as a valid substitute for the original?

39-8. The method for processing check payments using an image of the check captured during the sale and transmitted as a substitute for the original document is known as _____.

39-9. Remote deposit capture is also commonly referred to as _____.

39-10. True or False: The ACH network can be used to process any check drawn on a U.S. bank.

39-11. True or False: Check 21 has a maximum transaction amount cap of $25,000.

39-12. One method of risk mitigation when accepting checks at the point of sale is to compare the check writer's _____ to a national database of individuals with negative check writing history.

39-13. The image of a check used as a substitute for the original in a Check 21 transaction is known as an IRD, which stands for _____.

39-14. True or False: Check 21 processing can be used for recurring "bill pay" services.

39-15. True or False: A consumer must be notified that his check will be processed electronically when using Check 21.

Discussion Topics/Notes

39-1.   True

39-2.   MICR

39-3.   Automated Clearing House

39-4.   ACH or Automated Clearing House

39-5.   NACHA or National Automated Clearing House Association

39-6.   1994

39-7.   The Check Clearing for the 21st Century Act

39-8.   Remote Deposit Capture (or Check 21)

39-9.   Check 21

38-10. False

39-11. False

39-12. Driver's license or bank account number

39-13. Image replacement document

39-14. False

39-15. False

40-1. What company created the current version of the gift card?

40-2. Why did Blockbuster create the gift card?

40-3. What company developed the gift card infrastructure?

40-4. Name, define, and explain the two gift card systems.

40-5. How are funds controlled in a "closed loop" arrangement where a chain or association is involved?

40-6. What card options does a merchant have?

40-7. Name some common prepaid cards.

40-8. List five basic gift card programs.

40-9. List four benefits of gift card sales for the merchant.

40-10. Studies show that customers with two services or more are _____ less likely to leave their current banking relationship.

40-11. Name some benefits of selling gift cards for ISOs and agents.

40-12. True or False: Once the gift card setup is completed, the work of the MLS is done.

40-13. True or False: The only time gift cards are needed is around Christmas.

40-14. How long before common gift buying events (Christmas, graduation, "Hallmark holidays") should merchants promote gift cards aggressively?

40-15. According to the editorial director of *Colloquy* magazine, Rick Ferguson, "A loyalty program is one that seeks to _____, _____, and _____ the yield from customers through long-term, interactive, value-added relationships."

40-16. What year was the first semblance of a loyal program traced to?

40-17. What company had a long-running, nationwide loyalty program and what was it called?

40-18. What reason does Smith attribute to the decision of American Airlines to create the AAdvantage loyalty program from its Sabre database in 1981?

40-19. Name some programs that are available for loyalty/reward cards.

40-20. Name five benefits of a loyalty/rewards program.

40-21. True or False: Loyalty and reward programs are plug and play, just set them up and go.

40-22. List a few ideas and suggestions for merchants to keep their programs running smoothly.

40-23. List three successful marketing strategies.

Discussion Topics/Notes

40-1. Blockbuster Entertainment in the mid 1990s

40-2. To combat the use of new color printers and copiers that were used to forge its gift certificates

40-3. NaBANCO

40-4. "Open loop" prepaid cards are branded with the major card brand logos. These are targeted toward merchants who are not concerned with limiting the purchaser to its store alone. "Close loop" cards are those within a narrowly defined business location, chain, or local association. These cards are sold only in the stores that accept them.

40-5. A central location is set up for ACH pooling. Funds for the gift card are transferred from the seller to the central location and then to redeeming location for the amount used.

40-6.
1. Predesigned cards
2. Logo card
3. Custom-designed cards

40-7.
- Standard gift card
- Card for merchant credit
- Corporate voucher program
- Single authorization card
- eGift card

40-8.
1. School lunch program cards
2. College and university card
3. Medical card
4. House account debit card
5. Automotive services card
6. Beauty services card
7. Coupon card
8. Golf course cards
9. Retirement and senior living communities
10. Association, community cards
11. Charity cards
12. Fundraising cards

40-9.

- Increased sales and cash flow
- Breakage and unredeemed balances (be advised, companies list these as outstanding liabilities and some may balk)
- Better tracking and reporting capabilities
- Reduces fraud and duplicate usage
- No cash return to customers (advise merchant to include this statement with the refund policy)
- Builds merchant brand awareness
- Ease of use and faster transactions
- Low cost of entry
- Attract new customers
- Higher purchase amounts
- Promotes impulse purchases

40-10. 33%, but less likely if he has outstanding gift cards

40-11.

- Leading with a service other than card processing
- Helps with appointment setting
- Differentiates you from agents selling solely on price
- Helps to increase sales and customer retention
- Promotes terminal upgrades and leases
- Offers merchant an additional product to gift card processing
- Builds confidence and helps an agent secure close and long-lasting relationships with merchants
- Increases opportunities for agents to receive referrals to other merchants seeking gift card solutions

40-12. False. A successful gift card program will create happy clients and additional sales of gift cards along with referrals to other merchants. Offer marketing tips to make the program successful.

40-13. False. The biggest timeframe for gift cards is November and December with 35%. That means that 65% or close to two thirds of gift card sales are not around Christmas, but for birthdays, anniversaries, and graduations.

40-14. Two weeks

40-15. Identify, maintain, and increase

40-16. 1793

40-17. Sperry and Hutchinson Company, S&H Green Stamps

40-18. Because it costs significantly more to acquire a new customer than to market to an existing one. American Airlines had the advantage as it already had the list of fliers before it began the program.

40-19.
- Points reward program
- Dollar rewards
- Percentage rebate
- Discount rebate
- Frequency rewards program
- Combo card program

40-20.
1. Enhanced image/brand reinforcement
2. Promotes increased spending and repeat business
3. Ability to capture customer information and track purchase history
4. Tracking and reporting capabilities allow the merchant to easily manage the program
5. Creates a more personal relationship between the customer and the merchant
6. Distinguishes the merchant's business from the competition
7. Card members are more likely to refer others to visit
8. Targeted promotions or special events can be launched using cards
9. Solutions are affordable yet offer robust functionality to manage programs
10. Better return on investment than traditional marketing programs
11. Reduce labor cost and provide a streamlined process at the point of sale

40-21. False. If not properly promoted and used appropriately, it can alienate customers

40-22.
- Make sure the staff is educated on how the program works
- Incent sales clerks to push the program
- Make sure the merchant is not afraid to be mobile in the choice of programs
- Use the registration pages
- Communicate with customers regularly
- Ask customers for feedback
- Remind the merchant that he can have other things other than loyalty or rewards on cards
- Use social media to promote

40-23.
1. Relationship card marketing
2. Transactional card marketing
3. Shop local/community chamber of commerce
4. Frequency card marketing
5. Enforced card marketing
6. One-to-one card marketing
7. Punch card marketing
8. Text message marketing
9. Cellular and smartphone marketing

41-1. What are the three consequential differences between merchant card processing and ATMs referenced by the author?

41-2. What is Bauer's advice about ATM equipment price sheets and sales efforts to your prospect regarding equipment options?

41-3. What hardware options do most operators or locations focus their attention on?

41-4. Why is it so important to have a good system and/or understand the new account application process?

41-5. Bauer discusses three basic deal structures. What are they?

41-6. Why might focusing solely on giving more Interchange or surcharge revenue be a
        bad idea and what information in this chapter can be used to increase the value
        for a client?

41-7. Bauer mentions "choose your provider wisely" several times. What does he mean
        and why is this so important?

41-8. What does an ISO base pricing on?

41-9. When should you share more residual/work with your ISO?

41-10. When should you walk away from a deal?

41-11. What type of competition can I expect?

Discussion Topics/Notes

41-1.
- The burden of physical cash logistics
- Reversed revenue streams (the acquirer is paid by the cardholder and the issuer with an ATM program, unlike POS where the acquirer pays the issuer)
- The physical labor and logistical necessities are greater with ATMs; they are not as mobile

41-2.   Focus only on the top three most popular models of ATMs at any given time; work with your ATM provider to identify which three makes/models this comprises.

41-3.
- Screens
- Lock type
- Cassette capacity and type
- Topper signage

41-4.   Professional documents that are neatly organized and a finely-tuned process for the sales process can help provide you with a competitive advantage. Facilitating the process as efficiently as possible will not only allow you to visit more prospects and sign-up more clients, it will instill confidence in your clients. A system that misses details and requires back-tracking will cost you time and resources, and you will lose the confidence of your prospect or client.

41-5.
1. Merchant owned and merchant filled
2. Investor or company owned and merchant loaded
3. Full-service placement

41-6.   Haggling over pennies with a merchant, operator, or your ATM provider over-simplifies everything that goes into driving and supporting a successful ATM. From a location's perspective, receiving the help needed, when it is needed, should always come paramount to receiving an extra nickel or even a quarter. Downtime at an ATM erases a few extra nickels really fast. At the same time, receiving payments and settlements on time and accompanied with an accurate statement, and having someone to answer your call if you have a question are value additions that not all providers do well. Focus on these items as well everything else discussed in this chapter to un-commoditize your ATM offering. Being more professional, starting with the proper ATM hardware options, followed by the paperwork and new-account process, will help set you apart from your competitors. Providing reports directly from the third-party processor is another small way to assure a merchant or operator that the information and payments are accurate. Ancillary products mentioned are additional ways to add value, such as branding, advertising, additional transaction types, couponing, etc.

41-7. ATM provider essentially means an ATM ISO, or expert working closely with an ISO, who has all of the resources, knowledge, relationships, documents, and systems to support and aid in the growth of an ATM sales channel. The ATM provider can not only help provide economies of scale, but also build a program to support your endeavor properly. Educational resources and marketing assistance are valuable to a young and growing channel, and the right provider can help with this. Earning the most on every deal might not be the best, especially if there is no direction or assistance to win a deal. Likewise, without the proper formula of support to the account after the sale, it could not only cost you the loss of the ATM business but maybe your core business with the account as well.

41-8. Volume and workload

41-9. When the workload may be too much or is out of your expertise area. Be sure the value is appropriate.

41-10. When the margin is not enough to cover the work and time that the account will likely require

41-11. It is a heavily saturated market. Competitors may offer deals to merchants where it is not profitable. Some make offers they cannot back or sustain.

42-1. Define 1099 and W2 classifications for agents and the advantages and disadvantages to an ISO.

42-2. What are the three IRS tests to determine an employer's degree of control?

42-3. True or False: Requiring an agent to rent space and phone, pay expenses, and sign an Independent Contractor Agreement is all that is needed to have the IRS recognize the arrangement as that of an independent contractor.

42-4. Name the four "behavioral control factors" according to the IRS website.

42-5. How can an ISO provide training classes or materials to ICs without violating the "behavioral control factors?"

42-6. What is the likely result of requiring the following of 1099 agents:
- When and where to do the work
- What tools or equipment to use
- What workers to hire or to assist with the work
- Where to purchase supplies and services
- What work must be performed by a specified individual
- What order or sequence to follow when performing the work

42-7. True or False: Only those ISOs who are registered with the card brands may market services under their own name.

42-8. Why is the practical application of the marketing rule complicated?

42-9. How can agents who represent multiple ISOs minimize exposure to fines?

42-10. True or False: Since sub ISOs must represent themselves as their primary ISO, this may cause issues for the primary ISO.

42-11. To be liable as a principal for the agent or sub ISO, what factors generally must be present?

42-12. List the possible reasons why a merchant will include the primary ISO in a lawsuit claiming liability for "ostensible agent."

42-13. For what additional problems does the ISO face potential liability?

42-14. What does Rianda suggest to help deflect liability claims?

42-15. What is the primary reason to set up as a corporation or limited liability company (LLC)?

42-16. Generally speaking, which form of incorporation is least desirable to a small business?

42-17. Where should you incorporate your business and why?

42-18. What is the cost of incorporating?

42-19. What legal protection do you have if you fail to properly form and/or maintain your corporation?

42-20. In what case would an agent have responsibility for a loss to the ISO?

42-21. What is one consequence to the sales agent for not being a party to the merchant agreement?

42-22. Does the agent have the right to sell the residual stream or the merchant account?

42-23. What are some differences between a no-risk ISO and an agent relationship?

42-24. List four reasons to be wary about signing up for a BIN relationship.

42-25. List three advantages of a BIN relationship.

42-26. What is the result of stepping from an agent relationship to a no-risk ISO or from a no-risk ISO to a BIN relationship too early?

42-27. Why does Rianda recommend negotiating the effective date when selling a portfolio?

42-28. Explain a Liquidated Damages Provision.

42-29. True or False: With a $5,000 Liquidated Damages Provision, you could face a $5,000 fine for moving a merchant with a $10 residual.

42-30. True or False: The agent needs to only focus on the multiple when selling a portfolio.

42-31. Define and explain claw-back provisions as they pertain to portfolio sales.

What solution is there to the brands' requirement that only registered ISOs can market under the brands' names with the implied "Ostensible Agency" liability such branding can bring?

42-1. A 1099 agent is an independent contractor. He can work for several ISOs and his income is solely based on production. The independent contractor is solely responsible for his own success or failure.

       The IC is attractive to ISOs for tax purposes (no withholding taxes, matching FICA, or worker's compensation or unemployment). Plus there are no training and support costs.

       Disadvantages to the ISO are the lack of controls over that agent. Cutting ties are dependent upon the specific contract between the parties. The ISO cannot mandate hours, number of contacts, or training for the agent.

       A W2 agent is an employee of the ISO. This is primarily an exclusive relationship. Advantages for the ISO are the abilities to dictate rules, quotas, and processes to the employee. There are set office hours and the employer has access to CRM records generated by the employee.

       Disadvantages are the taxation issues and employment law compliance.

42-2.
1. Behavioral
2. Financial
3. Type of relationship

42-3. False, it does not account for behavioral rules.

42-4.
1. Type of instruction given
2. Degree of instruction
3. Evaluation systems
4. Training

42-5. ISOs have the option of giving materials or recommending them at the agent's expense, but cannot require the agent to read, purchase, or participate.

42-6. If ever contested by an agent or the IRS, these practices will result in agents being classified as employees and result in fines and back tax levies. Plus the agents can sue for wage and hour violations, minimum wage, and overtime.

42-7. True. According to the rules of the brands, the identified ISO must be registered.

42-8. Many sub ISOs represent multiple ISOs and it would be awkward to have multiple materials with each ISO represented.

42-9. Market under the main ISO business is sent to.

42-10. True. Through "ostensible agency," the primary ISO may have legal liability for acts of the sub ISO and its agents.

42-11. The business owner dealing with the agent must believe in the agent's authority, and the belief must be reasonable.
   • The belief must be generated by some act or neglect of the principal sought to be charged.
   • The business owner, in relying on the agent's authority, must not be guilty of negligence.

42-12.
   • Agent presented himself as the primary ISO.
   • Agent's business card and marketing materials are in the name of the primary ISO.
   • Merchant contract is with the primary ISO and the bank.
   • In general, the contact numbers and customer support are of the primary ISO.

42-13. Sales agents who use fraudulent or deceitful means or make unauthorized changes to the contract

42-14. Add an area to the contract that identifies the sales agent as an independent agent of the ISO. ISOs could also change templates on business cards and marketing materials indicating that the agent or sub ISO is an independent agent.

42-15. To avoid personal liability for debts and obligations of the business

42-16. The C Corporation

42-17. You should incorporate in the state in which you operate. The seemingly advantageous reasons for incorporating in Delaware and Nevada do not apply to small businesses and if you do incorporate there, you will also need to register in your state as a foreign corporation.

42-18. The cost of incorporation varies by state. Michigan is $50; some are $100–$150. There are also tax considerations.

42-19. You will have no protection from liability.

42-20. Where the sales agent is complicit in the activities that caused the loss

42-21. The sales agent lacks the contractual protections enjoyed by the bank and the ISO.

42-22. The agent can expect (and negotiate) the right to sell his residual stream, but the merchant accounts are owned by the bank and ISO named on the contract.

42-23.
- The no-risk ISO will generally register with MasterCard and Visa so that it can market under its own name.
- The no-risk ISO typically receives a larger split due to its volume.
- The no-risk ISO may have to commit to production guarantees.
- The no-risk ISO typically handles customer service calls.

42-24.
1. Responsible for all merchant losses
2. Monitors risk
3. Substantial payment or line of credit as reserve for potential merchant losses
4. Minimum of 1,000 accounts needed per month for profit and operational efficiencies

42-25.
1. Typically better pricing—access to true Interchange
2. Underwriting (can accept some risk)—caution though, this is double-edged sword
3. Can control other merchant fees to enhance income stream

42-26. A costly investment in infrastructure and unnecessary exposure

42-27. To ensure the agent is paid residuals while he owned the stream

42-28. Language in the contract that allows the buyer to fine the seller for actions like violating the non-solicitation provision.

42-29. True

42-30. False. Payment schedule and contract language are also very important.

42-31. Claw-back provisions are similar to attrition guarantees. Where attrition guarantees involve not getting paid a delayed portion of the purchase price, a clawback involves a repayment of some percentage of the original purchase price.